LIFTING HIM UP

LIFTING HIM UP

Ron Kenoly &
Dick Bernal

NELSON WORD LIMITED

First published in the U.S.A. by Creation House Strang
Communications Company, Florida.

This edition published by Nelson Word Limited, Milton Keynes,
England.

ISBN 1-86024-460-2

Unless otherwise noted, all Scripture quotations are from the New
King James Version of the Bible. Copyright © 1979, 1980, 1982 by
Thomas Nelson Inc., publishers.
Used by permission.

Scripture quotations marked KJV are from the King James Version of
the Bible.

Scripture quotations marked NAS are from the New American
Standard Bible. Copyright 1960, 1962, 1963, 1968, 1971, 1972,
1973, 1975, 1977 by the Lockman Foundation.
Used by permission

Scripture quotations marked NIV are from the Holy Bible, New
International Version. Copyright © 1973, 1978, 1984, International
Bible Society. Used by permission.

Reproduced and printed in Great Britain for Nelson Word Ltd., by Cox
and Wyman Ltd., Reading.

Cover photograph: Courtesy of Paul Yates.

96 97 98 99 / 10 9 8 7 6 5 4 3 2

Contents

Preface

Late in 1944 two baby boys were born, one to black parents in Coffeyville, Kansas and the other to white parents in Watsonville, California. Born during a great worldwide war, little did their parents realise these precious bundles of joy would grow up to become front line leaders in the greatest war of all time—the final spiritual conflict between God and Satan.

It was forty-one years before the two men met, but

the events of their lives prepared them for their partnership in battle. Both boys, raised without a father, launched out on their own into the world at an early age. Each possessed natural gifts which they began to use in their late teen years. Ron Kenoly could sing—and sing well. His head was filled with original songs and music. His future seemed destined for the music world. Dick Bernal was a natural leader able to inspire others. His peers and leaders often called upon him to act as president, chairman or captain of one group or another. By the time both boys entered their twenties, their futures seemed secure.

Ron became a nightclub singer and recording artist. The entertainment mecca of Los Angeles provided him with recording contracts, gigs and all the right connections.

Dick's business acumen gained the attention of a large steel company, and he worked his way into a leadership position before the age of twenty-six. Life looked good for both of them, but neither allowed room for God in their lives.

Ron's childhood days of being raised in a church environment seemed far removed from his present lifestyle. Dick had never attended church and didn't want to. His grandmother's discipline seemed quite adequate to help him figure out right from wrong along life's bumpy path. But as the confusing sixties gave way to the selfish seventies, both men, through the prayers and encouragement of their wives, Tavita Kenoly and Carla Bernal, found God and accepted His plan for their lives. As they entered the eighties they also entered a covenant relationship that led to the merging of their lives and ministry. Read on as Ron and Dick share their stories and show us a greater understanding of how we can lift up Jesus in our worship.

Section I

by Ron Kenoly

Acknowledgements

I thank God for His mercy and patience. It took a long time to learn some of the lessons He taught me. I am confident He will complete that which He has begun in me.

Tavita, I thank God for you. I don't know where I would be without you. Your encouragement and love has helped to keep me focused and committed to the things that God has called me to do.

Thanks to my mum, Edith Kenoly. You have always believed in me and have never stopped praying for me.

My sons, Tony, Ronald and Sam, you are my inspiration. Thanks for sharing me with the body of Christ.

Thanks to my pastors, Dick and Carla Bernal, and to the members and staff of Jubilee for your love, teaching and prayers.

Mike Coleman, Don Moen and the family at Integrity Music, thank you for allowing me to partner with you to establish God's glory through praise and worship.

Thanks to Stephen Strang, Creation House, and Tessie Guell for her help in writing. You have really blessed my life, and I love you.

Thanks to the staff of Ron Kenoly Ministries, past and present, and to the volunteers and friends along the way. I love you all.

Introduction

*E*venings in the San Francisco Bay area are notoriously cool, but this summer night was sweltering. With his head bowed and his big shoulders hunched in dejection, Ron Kenoly made his way to the little Foursquare church on the corner of 64th Avenue and Bancroft Boulevard.

Slipping into the empty church, he stepped inside the hushed sanctuary and made his way down the aisle. 'Is God still interested in my music?' he wondered.

Although secular record labels were clamouring for his talent, Christian companies had ignored his requests for an audition. Was it possible that his music career ended the day he rededicated his life to the Lord?

Sitting down at the piano, Kenoly began playing the few worship choruses he knew. Surrounded by empty pews in the deserted church, he offered up to God the music that was in his heart.

When the 'concert' was over, a new man emerged from a pool of tears. From that night on Ron Kenoly knew that he was called to perform for an audience of one—God and God alone.

That is how *Charisma* magazine described my 'concert for One' that August evening in 1982. I could not have expressed it better because there are some experiences in life that you cannot find the words to describe by yourself. That evening was a turning point in my life.

Looking back, it's amazing and humbling for me to see all that the Lord has done. God takes delight in making beautiful things out of foolish things, and even though I wouldn't call myself beautiful I am in awe of what He has done with my life.

Writing this book with Pastor Dick is an honour for me. My desire is that those who read this book will grow deeper in their relationship with the Lord and that the principles presented here would bring them into a fuller knowledge of God's presence.

My relationship with Pastor Dick, who is not only my pastor, but my friend, has taught me the importance of the relationship between a pastor and a music leader. I believe this is one of the most important relationships within the church and consequently one that has suffered great attacks from the enemy. Even though I'll expand on this particular subject later, allow me to say here that it is my heart's burden to see the relationship between pastors and music leaders be restored to its proper place in the body of Christ. I pray God can also use this book in that capacity.

1

The Power of God's Presence

When I became a Christian I knew in principle I could touch the heart of God in worship, but in August of 1982 I realised that fact when I went to the church and did the concert for God. When I walked out of the church that night I knew God was smiling on me and that I had pleased Him.

I had worshipped many times before, but I think

what made that night special is that 100 per cent of my attention was on God.

Other times when I was part of a worship team or when I led worship, there were so many distractions: making sure we were playing right, trying to think of the right words to exhort the audience and so on.

What keeps us from putting all our attention on the Lord is the fear of man. We are concerned about what the person next to us is going to think or say. People who truly enter into worship don't care about those around us. All they know is they are with God and that if there are any problems God will take care of them.

I changed some of my schedules and ways of thinking so I could come to a new place in worshipping the Lord. *I entered into the Lord's presence.* It was a place I had never gone before. I realised nothing else is more important than being in His presence. After going there then you are compelled to take someone else there—you want everyone to know what it's like.

I know the kind of feeling the Samaritan woman had after she talked to Jesus. She ran to the city and told everybody, 'Come see this man. He knows about me. He knows everything I have ever done' (see John 4:29). Something special had just happened to her—she had been with God!

The role of worship in the life of the believer is indispensable. It is the most important thing—the ultimate thing—a believer can do. The act of worship develops and deepens a relationship with God. It's the one thing everyone can do without exception because it's a matter of turning your heart towards the Lord and yielding to Him and listening for His voice.

Five Events of Worship

I believe at least five events take place during our time of worship. To discover them, let's look at Isaiah's commission.

> At the sound of their voices the doorposts and thresholds shook and the temple was filled with smoke. 'Woe to me!' I cried. 'I am ruined! For I am a man of unclean lips, and I live among a people of unclean lips, and my eyes have seen the King, the Lord Almighty.'
>
> Then one of the seraphs flew to me with a live coal in his hand, which he had taken with tongs from the altar. With it he touched my mouth and said, 'See, this has touched your lips; your guilt is taken away and your sin atoned for.'
>
> Then I heard the voice of the Lord saying, 'Whom shall I send? And who will go for us?' And I said, 'Here am I. Send me!' He said, 'Go and tell this people: "Be ever hearing, but never understanding; be ever seeing, but never perceiving" ' (Is. 6:4-9, NIV).

Let's look at the five events that occur when we enter into God's presence.

1. We respond or allow ourselves to be found by the Lord.

Isaiah allowed himself to be found by God. Jesus said the Father was seeking worshippers (see John 4:23). Like Isaiah you have to allow yourself to be found.

2. We actively yield to His lordship and His beckoning.

We do that through physical expression and emotional expression. We lift our hands or kneel down; putting ourselves in that yielded position.

3. We declare His lordship.

We speak out words of love, thankfulness, adoration, exaltation and declare His power. The things we confess establish what we believe. This is evident in Isaiah's writing.

4. We receive His forgiveness.

This can be divided into two parts. First, we are convicted and cleansed. As we worship, the Lord will often convict us of sin, but He cleanses us as soon as we ask forgiveness. Too often we carry guilt that God wants to release us from. We come right up to Him but refuse to release our baggage.

We must learn to allow Him to bless us, which occurs when we allow ourselves to be cleansed.

Second, we see ourselves through His eyes. God does not see our filthy rags any longer. He sees the robes of righteousness that He has draped around our shoulders (see Is. 61:10). We do not have to come into the throne room hanging our heads. The King has invited us to come in as His honoured guests. Forgiveness has a great side effect–joy. In His presence there is fullness of joy (see Ps. 16:11).

5. We respond to His mandate.

Isaiah made himself available, and the Lord gave him a mandate to speak and prophesy to the people. We begin to see that we are victorious and can do all things through Christ. Then we realise we can go and accomplish His mandate for us as a body and as individuals, because He makes us more than conquerors.

Corporate and Private Worship

We can enter into God's presence in two different settings: private and corporate.

Corporate worship happens when two or more gather in His name and acknowledge His presence. Whenever we are in a public setting we need to be courteous towards other people we are worshipping with. What we do as individuals may be inappropriate in corporate worship because it would bring a distraction to someone else's worship time.

Though I believe we need to worship the Lord in freedom and without inhibitions, I'm also a firm believer in balance. Generally speaking, I think we have used 'freedom' as an excuse for wrong behaviour, and we have blamed a lot of things on the Spirit of God that were born in the flesh. Paul said everything needs to be done 'decently and in order' (1 Cor. 14:40, KJV).

If the way I praise God in a public setting is going to interfere with your sincere attempt to worship the Lord, then there's a conflict there. This is how I reason it out: Why would the Holy Spirit ask me to do something that would interfere with someone else's ability to worship? Even though the body is composed of individual parts, those parts need to work together in order for the body to function properly and accomplish its purposes.

God has raised up a body that needs to come together as one. Worshipping the Lord together builds unity in the church.

Private worship is the primary way you develop your relationship with the Lord. It is where you can fine tune your ear to hear His voice. It is where He will whisper secrets and share His heart with you.

Also keep in mind that there is a special way in which only *you* can touch God's heart. You are a unique individual created by Him and only you can worship Him like you do. There is a special place in

God's heart that only you can fill through your worship time alone with Him.

The same applies to corporate worship, there is a way in which a church fills God's heart. Every church has a special purpose in God's plans. It does not matter if it's a small congregation or a church of five thousand members—there is some special project that each church is called to do, special people that each church is called to reach out to.

And just like we have corporate mandates, things the Lord calls us to do as a body—we also have individual mandates—things you were born to do that neither I or anyone else for that matter can fulfil.

It is in the place of intimate worship that the Lord gives us many of those mandates. Enter in and find out what special things He wants you and your church to do.

2

Into His Presence

The function of a worship leader is to bring other people into God's presence. I am often asked how I know when I have accomplished my job. The truth is that it's not something I see with the natural eye. I do not have a written formula. Sometimes I know I'm finished when I can feel the presence of the Lord in the room so strong that I know the only thing left for me to do is to get out of God's way. Many times it is not appropriate for me to say or do anything.

When I get to the place where I know that it's no longer me leading the people, but the Spirit of the Lord, I know they are there. The Scriptures describe that happening at Solomon's dedication of the temple.

> The trumpeters and singers joined in unison, as with one voice, to give praise and thanks to the Lord...Then the temple of the Lord was filled with a cloud...for the glory of the Lord filled the temple of God (2 Chr. 5:13-14).

Notice how the verse said the people were 'joined in unison'. They were all in one accord mentally, spiritually and emotionally. At those times, I know God is working among His people, His family. That's when I just get out of His way. I have done my job.

However, all this is not to say that we should avoid planning. We must organise because we are diverse people and when we come together in worship we need unity among us. Music is one of those unifying things. It is a vehicle, and it helps us get our minds off distractions and problems. The worship leader should plan music that will unify the body of Christ in order to help usher in His presence.

Prerequisites for a Worship Leader

I am a firm believer that it is important to minister *to* Him so we can adequately minister *for* Him. The Lord has confirmed this to me many times. One scripture that I believe supports this idea is Matthew 6:33:

> But seek first his kingdom and his righteousness, and all these things will be given to you as well.

Though Jesus is talking specifically about provision in this verse, I also believe He is describing a spiritual principle about worship. To me, 'all these things will be given to you as well' represents Him giving me the proper setting to lead others into worship. The prerequisite is for me to first come into His kingdom myself.

Jesus lived out this principle in His own life. We see it described in His prayer for the disciples:

> Righteous Father, though the world does not know you, *I know you*, and they know that you have sent me. *I have made you known to them*, and will continue to make you known (John 17:25, italics added).

A worship leader must spend time with the Father and find out what the Father wants them to do. Then the worship leader can bring the congregation into the awareness of the presence of God. Once that happens the Spirit can do things like healing, deliverance, revelation and more. Everything that He does is going to be good. At that point the worship leader has become a facilitator.

To bring others into God's presence, I must know them and be a leader they can trust. That is the way of a good shepherd. Jesus said, 'I am the good shepherd; I know my sheep and my sheep know me' (John 10:14). When people know that I love them, then I can be a leader for them.

For instance, when I was in South Korea, the people in the area where I ministered were not very expressive in their singing. But when it came to praying or singing in the Spirit they just released everything! I had never seen people pray with such fervour or intensity.

As a worship leader I had to adjust to the needs of the Koreans and realise that their expressions of worship are different from mine. If I would not have been able to realise this, then a cultural difference would have become a worship obstacle. I might have tried to get a response from them which they could not give. I would have been frustrated and quenched the Spirit, instead of assisting His work.

We can get used to seeing things one way, and we can misread what is going on or think God is not doing something. The truth is, God does things in different ways, in different places, with different people.

I used to get annoyed by people who clearly had no intention to worship or get involved. Thank God I have been delivered, and those people don't bother me anymore. We should lead those who follow. I do not worry about those who will not follow. I know where I am going. If they want to follow me great, if not, that's fine too. I have found the best way to lead worship is to concentrate on getting into God's presence, and then those around you will be naturally attracted.

In a recent worship service in Pennsylvania there was an old lady sitting right up front and she was visibly not getting involved. The look on her face told me she was just putting up with it. At the end of the service the Lord put in my heart a song I was not planning to do. I began to sing the hymn: *What a Friend We Have in Jesus.* I made my way down to her as I was singing, and I grabbed her hands. I kept singing, 'Oh! what a friend we have in Jesus.'

It was obvious during the meeting that even though she wanted to participate, she was apathetic to contemporary worship. To put it simply I was just not 'walking down her street'. All of a sudden her entire countenance changed, and she became a child. It was a total release for her. Tears running down her face, hands lifted high, it was as if there was no one in that place except her and the Lord. You could visibly see the change in her.

Sometimes it is the entire congregation that needs to hear something specific. A few years ago I was with Worship International, in a small town near Houston, Texas. Worship International, the non-profit arm of

Integrity Music, had organised a worship seminar and I was to speak and lead worship for two evenings. The place only held about twelve hundred people, which is smaller than the usual meeting space for these seminars. So Worship International decided to charge a minimal sitting fee in order to have some kind of crowd control. We did not want people to drive miles and miles and then find that they could not get in.

The place was packed. The problem is that in paying the sitting fee, people came in with a concert mentality. And let me tell you the concert attitude is drastically different from the praise and worship attitude.

The concert mentatlity says, 'I paid admission, now you owe me. You better sing the songs I want to hear, sing the high notes, do the fancy dance and put on a great show.' The worship mentality is completely opposite, the worship leader is not there to put on a show, but to lead people into God's presence. He is there to give the people what God wants, not what the audience wants. God is not interested in entertaining them or performing for them, but rather in performing a work in their lives and hearts.

After I had been on for fifteen minutes I realised people were just staring at me with this 'impress me' look. So I changed the whole order of service and started doing some songs that were not on the list and that we had not practiced at all. They still seemed unresponsive. Finally I stopped everything, and I shared with them the difference between a concert mentality and worship mentality. I said, 'I have come to worship the Lord with you, and that is what I intend to do. If there is a way in which I can help you enter God's presence and get involved, I will. But I could not care less if you like me or my "performance". I want to minister to the Lord and you can come with me. As King David said, "Oh! Magnify the Lord with me and let us exalt His name together." And take me off any pedestal you have me on because I don't deserve it. I am just like you, and I need to worship the Lord too.'

I started singing a song everyone knew, *Yes, Jesus loves me, the Bible tells me so*. The whole place filled with God's presence, and His Spirit started moving among the people. We did only about a third of the songs that had been rehearsed, but the spirit of worship that filled that place was amazing!

We saw the power of God move in a tremendous way. All it took was sensitivity to the Lord and people yielding their hearts to His voice. Friends, in all we do, not just in worship, we need to, we must, learn to set aside all the things that hinder us from coming into His presence, and we should give Him our undivided hearts.

3

Avoiding the
Lucifer Spirit

The Lucifer spirit, from my perspective, is the spirit of an individual who, because of his talent and abilities, begins to think he is more important than he really is. This happens a lot with associate pastors and worship leaders. It's especially common when the worship leaders' gifts and abilities are a little more polished (according to the world's standards) than those of the people who have authority over them.

For instance, let us look at Moses. Moses was not a great speaker. He did not want to speak because he knew he stammered in getting the message across. So his brother Aaron was called to go along with him and speak for him.

We see the Lucifer spirit at work when Moses went to the mountain and Aaron stayed behind with the people. What happened? There was rebellion in the ranks and though the Scripture is not very clear I am sure part of the struggle was Aaron wondering why he had to obey Moses, when he was the one who did all the talking. Aaron allowed the words of the people to manipulate him (see Ex. 32).

The Lucifer Spirit Divides

I have seen cases where singers are better speakers than senior pastors. As a result they allow themselves to receive and hang on to the flattery of the people. Those compliments only make matters worse. They feed the idea that they are better than those in authority over them. Then they start using their popularity to manipulate and establish their own agenda, which could be contrary to the mandate given by the Lord to the senior pastor. We see then how the Lucifer spirit can manifest as someone who wants to take over and gain control because they think they can do a better job.

I have seen it more times than I would like to

admit. Often the result is a church split, which is not the way God wants to multiply the body of Christ. The Lord will still work despite the circumstances, but the individual in the centre of the problem needs to go out with a blessing not a curse. When God sends someone out He does it in order and with the blessing of the congregation. However, the opposite was true when God cast Lucifer from heaven. He did not give His blessing because Lucifer's actions were born out of rebellion.

We see where Lucifer made all those mistakes in Ezekiel 28. It was his responsibility to maintain the attitude of praise and worship around the throne. God had given him great talents and abilities, and Lucifer had all the resources he needed to accomplish the job he was created for. But when he decided everything he did was good and decided to take over, his pride got in the way, and he fell. His iniquity was making plans to overthrow God.

We see another example in the account of Herod's death. God made Herod king, but the proud Herod would not give the glory to God. The Bible says an angel of the Lord struck him down, he was eaten by worms and died (see Acts 12:21-23).

Keep Ego in Check

You may be thinking that this all sounds like the sin of pride, and you are partially right. Pride is bound up in the Lucifer spirit. Pride is haughtiness and it exalts oneself.

Personally, by God's grace I have never had to deal with the pride of the Lucifer spirit. But I have dealt with that which can lead to pride if not kept in check—ego.

Society has a distorted image of the word ego. Webster's dictionary defines ego as the self. Ego, or the self, can be sanctified for God's purpose. It is knowing and being confident in what you are capable of doing. If the ego is left uncontrolled and not sanctified, it leads to pride. It is one thing to be confident of what you can do through Christ and another to do them in your own strength and not give God the glory. In other words, when we do not acknowledge the Lord our ego gets twisted and becomes the sin of pride.

The ego can be salvaged and used for the glory of God. The apostle Paul had a big ego: he was a well - educated individual with an impressive Jewish bloodline who had a lot of things going for him (Acts 22:3). He was confident of his abilities.

When he encountered Jesus he did not let go of his confidence. He simply gave all his abilities to the service of the Lord. He never lorded his abilities over anybody, but he was confident of those things God had placed in his life. In all his teachings, in all the things he did, we see that he was confident.

In my case, I am confident of what the Lord has called me to do. I am a worship leader. I know He has blessed me with a good singing voice. He has given me experiences that have brought me to the place where I am in my life. I know I am a good worship leader, but I am not the best. There are many who I admire and I know are better worship leaders than me. However, that does not stop me from knowing that I am a good worship leader. I also know that my motives are right, that I love God's people and that I want them to experience God's presence.

When I see myself through God's eyes, not mine, I say, 'Yes! I can!' With His strength and help and by His grace I can do all things through Christ who strengthens me! (Phil. 4:13). That is redeemed ego: I know who I am in Christ, and I know what I can do! But, I still bring my wisdom, my talents, my knowledge and my experiences to the foot of the cross because I know that it is only by Him that I can do all those things.

Friend, be confident in God's calling on your life. Not doing so gives the enemy an open door to bring you down. If the enemy can get you to doubt your identity in Christ and in His ability to do with you what He purposes to do, then the enemy has won.

4

Birthing a Song

One area that can be of particular frustration for some people is writing songs. I am often asked how I write songs or if there are times when I sit down to write a song and nothing comes.

The truth is songwriting is easy for me, and I almost never have songwriters' block. I believe songwriting is a skill just like building a house is a skill. Your materials can be your Bible, sermons, life experiences, catchy phrases, dictionaries and a thesaurus.

You also need to consider who you are writing for. If you are writing for a general congregation then the vocal range has to be limited, if you are writing for someone like Matthew Ward then you can be creative and write a song that would showcase his incredible range and singing ability.

In my experience there are three ways songs come. They come by personal inspiration. These songs are born after you see or experience something that inspires you to write. Songs also come by request. These songs are written when a pastor, leader or any other individual asks you to write a song with a specific theme for a specific occasion. I have written many songs born out of Pastor Dick's messages. Finally, there are songs that come by divine inspiration. These are the songs that come straight from the throne, and you are afraid to take credit for them.

Jesus is Alive is one of these divinely inspired songs. It came about in 1987 when I was trying to write a title song for a musical I had written. I did not feel like any of the songs I already had could be used as a title song. I was writing in my house during a personal devotional time. All of a sudden the music and lyrics for *Jesus is Alive* started running through my mind, and I wrote out the whole song in ten minutes. I did not have to change or modify anything.

This does not mean that only those songs which are directly inspired by God are the more anointed ones. A passage of Scripture you read may spark a personal inspiration song. In the same way, if the inspiration is your pastor's teachings, that also is the word of God. Indirectly, all songs are inspired by God, since it is Jesus and His Holy Spirit who dwells in you. He will bless your efforts.

Selecting Songs

Whether or not he writes songs, a worship leader at any level knows what it is like to select songs. It requires the same kind of planning and inspiration as writing the songs yourself!

If you are leading worship in a church service, it is essential to find out what the pastor is going to talk about. For instance, Pastor Dick often preaches messages in a series. Let us say he is on a series about spiritual warfare. Then I know I have to locate all the spiritual warfare songs I can find and choose from there. I would choose songs such as *Making War in the Heavenlies*, *Victory in Jesus* and *Going Up to the High Places*.'

After you have communicated with the pastor, take into consideration the congregation. You would not use the same songs in a youth group meeting that you would use in an elderly group meeting. Sometimes the type of service and the time frame also have a lot to do with song selection. A Friday night service with no time limitations is very different from a Sunday morning service that is being televised. However, at all times the bottom line is getting people into the presence of God. The worship leader must assist them in getting their minds and hearts into a place where they can see all that God has for them.

Too many worship leaders have fallen into a rut of picking five praise songs and five worship songs. But the same pattern does not work all the time. A worship leader is more than a song leader. They need to be in tune with the Holy Spirit and move according to His leading. If during one particular song it is obvious that the Lord is moving, don't move on to the next song because the schedule tells you to. Stay with God, and if you have to stay with that one song and forget about singing the next three, then do it!

I also think that in many charismatic circles we have gone overboard with praise songs that sing *about* God rather than *to* God. We don't place enough emphasis on worship time that allows intimacy with the Lord. We can sing praise songs and not have fellowship with God. Worship begins when we become intimate with Him. Praise is what takes us into a place where we can worship the Lord.

Special Songs

I believe one of the responsibilities of the worship leader is to reinforce the pastor's teaching. That is why I encourage worship leaders to write songs that reinforce what their pastor preaches.

A pastor can only preach that sermon one time to the same congregation, but it may be a message that the people need to hear again and live with it. As humans, we learn by repetition and redundancy. That is where the songs come in and reinforce what the pastor taught. The more we rehearse a thing in our minds the more we begin to believe it and act upon it.

As we begin to sing the songs over and over again we relive that experience or message. Moses wrote a song about Israel's deliverance from Egypt so that the people could remember what God had done and teach it to generation after generation. Even today we have groups of people who pass along their history and heritage by singing songs. What richer heritage than that of Christ? What better message to sing?

As individuals and as congregations we all have special songs that mean a lot to us. Remember the song that was playing during your water baptism? Or when you received that special word from the Lord? Or when He reminded you of a promise? Or when He rebuked you, yet loved you so tenderly? All those songs serve as reminders of His faithfulness and as milestones the enemy cannot destroy.

When writing songs the bottom line is to allow the Lord to work through you. We are all the same in many ways, and what touches your heart is bound to touch many others. So let the praises in your heart overflow not only through your mouth, but through your hands.

5

Characteristics of a Worship Leader

Through the years I have observed similar characteristics among people who I consider good worship leaders. Before I share my observations with you, I want to make it clear that the decision of who becomes a worship leader rests with the Lord. He is the one who decides who is called to do what.

A Worship Leader is...

A worship leader is not just someone that leads

people in singing songs. Worship is the key word in worship leader. As we worship, this person helps usher us into the presence of the Lord. If you are serving the Lord as a worship leader or feel called to do so, the following five descriptions of what a worship leader is would apply to you:

1. A good student of the Word

Why? So that you can sing and lead songs that are in line with the Word. Every good or popular Christian song is not in line with God's Word. Many songs through the years have been unscriptural. They may have sounded good and blessed a lot of people, but that doesn't make them scriptural. The worship leader needs to be able to discern whether the material he is feeding the people is in line with the Scripture.

2. Radically saved by an experience with Jesus Christ

In other words, the leader needs to be Christian beyond a shadow of a doubt. An ability to lead others in prayer is a must because those in your worship group will come to you with all kinds of problems and situations. If you cannot deal with those things in prayer, those problems will be on your mind and their minds when you are supposed to be worshipping. The problems can create so much confusion that you cannot come before God. You cannot take the congregation to a place where you yourself cannot go. Every time that you come together, pray, 'Lord, we take this time to come before you and lay every thing down that would distract us from worshipping you.' Then you can go out and lead your congregation into the presence of the Lord.

3. A bold leader

If you are scared as you stand before the people, the spirit of fear and timidity will transfer right over to the congregation. People will never enter into worship. They need to have confidence that you know what you are doing. You need to lead with authority. When the clock says it is time to go, you need to be able to tell people when to sit down, stand up, get out of the aisle or stop talking. You need to be able to tell people it is time to worship.

In some churches, expressions in tongues can be distracting during the worship service. It might or might not be a word from the Lord. A worship leader must keep control of the situation and discern if it is the right time for a word. Be bold enough to interpret that word, demand that the one who gave the word interpret, or tell the person to be quiet and go see an elder to let him discern the word. Watch out for dancers becoming a distraction, whether in spirit or flesh. You need to have ushers take the person to the side. Take authority and lead.

4. A Skilled musician or singer

David appointed skilled musicians. That does not mean you need a degree in music, but to avoid bad notes and out-of-tune singing. If your music is bad then there will be a distraction and people will not enter into worship.

5. Submissive to authority

One of the biggest problems for pastors is worship leaders who have their own agenda. Worship leading is a subordinate ministry. God has placed pastors over us. There are worship leaders who lead better than the pastor preaches, but remember Lucifer. You cannot allow yourself to be puffed up. You will lead in music and usher in the presence of God, but the Lord will give the pastor a word for the people that will sustain them.

Learn who your pastor is, his personality. Choose songs to compliment him, perhaps his favourite songs, so that the pastor can enter into God's presence and then be anointed enabling him to preach. It motivates them in a special way. Be in agreement on plans. Keep him aware of challenges you are having with the music department. Keep in line with what he is preaching, reinforcing his message. Be loyal to your pastor. He needs to be assured of your loyalty. Build a unified relationship between you and your pastor. Build him up before the congregation.

Ten Things That Bother a Pastor About a Worship Leader

I have noticed <u>ten things that bother a pastor about a worship leader</u>. I've tried to avoid these things myself, and it has made my relationship with Pastor Dick much more fruitful.

1. Not starting on time

2. Not stopping on time

3. Talking too much before, during and after the worship time

4. Singing songs that are not appropriate for worship

5. Inappropriate apparel

6. Moving too far ahead of the people, and drifting off into your own world

7. Verbal abuse of the congregation when their response is not what you want

8. Singing at a pitch which is too high or too low for the congregation

9. Redundancy, singing the same songs week after week

10. Having your own agenda. Example: using your position as a stepping stone to a record contract.

Pastor Dick has shared with me ten things he has discovered through the years that bother a worship leader about a pastor. He has also tried very hard to avoid these things.

1. Lack of support from the pulpit (the pastor)

2. Cutting the flow of worship because of time constraints

3. A pastor (and wife) who do not enter into worship

4. Hearing all the problems with no praise for the good things

5. Being asked to do a number on the spot (very embarrassing when the worship team doesn't know it)

6. When the pastor's wife wants to run the department

7. Not sending the worship leader to seminars and conferences that would truly help the church

8. When money will not be spent for good musical equipment

9. Pastors who do not spend quality time with worship leaders to pray and counsel with them, especially in hard times

10. Pastors who do not trust the worship leader's judgement in building a first-rate team

These things are self-explanatory. However, if you are a worship leader I encourage you to prayerfully bring these things to the Lord. After you have done so, talk to your pastor and humbly ask him if he feels you are guilty of any of these things. If you are a pastor, examine your heart concerning your relationship with your worship leader.

By now you have read plenty about my relationship with Pastor Dick. Meeting and getting to know him as both a pastor and a friend has been one of God's great blessings on my life. I appreciate that he is somebody I don't have trouble submitting to. We have gone through a lot individually and together, yet he remains a man that leads with servanthood. Pastor, are you leading in a Godly manner that encourages others to submit to you?

My prayer is that these simple lists will serve as icebreakers to heal and improve many pastor/worship leader relationships.

6

God is Able

One of the most precious moments I have had in leading worship occurred in Atlanta, Georgia, during the recording of God is Able. That album has a song titled *Use Me*.

If You can use anything Lord,
You can use me.
Take my hands, Lord
And my feet,
Touch my heart, Lord
And speak through me.
If You can use anything
Lord, You can use me.*

I remember singing those words and thinking, *Oh, Lord! This is so true about my life.*

I had a successful career singing pop and soul numbers in night clubs. I had contracts with MCA, United Artists, Warner Brothers and A&M. Though I never had a blockbuster recording I had enough 'near hits' to make a good living. I had a good career and respect from the industry.

But all my success came at a huge price—my family. Tavita and I had a turbulent marriage for seven years, where there was a lot of physical, verbal and mental abuse that resulted in separation.

Then in the spring of 1975 our lives changed drastically. Tavita recommitted her life to the Lord during a service at First Baptist Church in Van Nuys. Not long after that she was baptised in the Holy Spirit at Angelus Temple, the famous Foursquare congregation in Los Angeles.

As a result we got back together. For me, the most obvious evidence of Tavita's new commitment was that she was no longer selfish. She began to submit in a way that she had not done before. She began to recognise me as the priest of our home, as the one ultimately responsible for the success of our marriage. Her prayer was, 'Lord, help me to see him through Your eyes.' She began to support God's plan for my life and acknowledge me as the husband she was believing God for, even before it had come to pass.

She was speaking in tongues, and I thought she had gone out of her mind. But I could see it was not about me. It was about her and the Lord, and I wanted to be a part of it.

It was 19 November, 1975, when I gave my life to the Lord. It was 8.30 a.m. and I was watching Pat Robertson on *The 700 Club*. A few years before I had been diagnosed with chronic spastic bronchitis, and this particular morning I was having a hard time breathing. Next thing I knew Robertson was calling me by name! He said, 'There is a man named Ronnie (which is what my mother calls me), and you are having trouble with your breathing. Receive healing from the Lord right now.'

By then I was not only ready for the touch, I was ready for the Lord! I realised what a mess I had made for myself, and I wanted the Lord to do for me what He had done for Tavita. On 20 November, Tavita and I went to the church to receive marriage counselling. It was also then I received the baptism of the Holy Spirit.

A New Life in Christ

The hardest part of starting a new life was letting go of my successful career. I tried to keep my secular career, but I could not. I needed a clean break so we gave up everything and moved to Oakland. I started working at the College of Alameda passing out towels in the locker room. It was a humbling time, but I was determined not to go back to my old ways. I started attending night school to earn my associate of arts degree in music.

I began writing Christian music and sending letters and demos to Christian labels. I never received any response, except one who wrote to say 'thanks, but no thanks'. At the same time I was receiving all sorts of offers from secular contacts and companies. But I was determined to stand firm.

After toiling in the locker room for eighteen months, I was called into the dean's office for an evaluation and promotion. When the dean started going through my file he was shocked to learn I had nine records released, songs on the charts and all sorts of musical accomplishments. The dean submitted my records to the California Board of Regents and I was issued credentials equivalent to a master's degree and a teaching licence. I immediately started teaching voice at the college.

Still, my desire was to sing. The summer of 1982 was a real low point in my life. But as much as I loved music, I loved God more. I could not go back to singing secular music even if it meant never singing again.

It was then I found myself having the 'concert for One'. And it was that night when I relinquished my dream and desire to become a recording artist.

After that turning point in my life I started receiving invitations to lead worship at other churches and events. Some of the great people of God who I had the honour to work with were Lester Sumrall, Jack Hayford and Ed Cole, among others. The support of these leaders led me to be hired by Mario Murillo to lead worship at his crusades.

Eventually, it was through Mario and other friends that I met Pastor Dick for a second time in 1985. (We met once before briefly in 1982.) He had started Jubilee Christian Centre in San Jose, California four years earlier, and he was looking for a worship leader. I started helping and in 1985 joined the church's full-time staff.

I will be honest with you, once in a while I thought of making hit records, but I was so happy and fulfilled in leading others in worship. I was fully content.

Submit to the Lord

But the Lord, in His awesome and eternal faithfulness had plans far greater than what I could have imagined. In 1990, Don Moen, Integrity Music's vice president, visited Jubilee after he had been encouraged by others to come and see how we led worship. After the second morning service Don walked up to me and asked if I wanted to record a praise and worship album for Integrity.

There are some things you don't have to pray about. That was one of them!

The rest is history. At the time I write this I have recorded four albums with Integrity and have signed an exclusive contract with them. It is not for my glory, but for His!

I realise you may have already heard or read this story. However, this is my chance to share the lesson to be learned behind my testimony.

In our Christian walk there is nothing greater than surrendering our lives—every aspect of them—to the Lord. It was not until I gave Him all my desires and dreams concerning music that He started opening doors. This is not because He is some big master sitting up in the sky who wants to beat us into submission. As a matter of fact I have witnessed Him doing things and using people that quite honestly puzzle me.

He does this because He knows better than we do what is good for us. He knows He can do infinitely greater things with our lives that we could ever dream or imagine. But in order to do that, He needs us in a surrendered, moldable state where our only preoccupation is Him. Please allow my testimony to be an example of this.

Today, I still struggle with breathing problems. It is a battle that I fight. I have had several doctors tell me they don't know how I am able to sing, but I have made up my mind that I will continue singing for the Lord. I have embraced Psalm 150 that says, 'Let everything that has breath praise the Lord.' So, I am going to give to God whatever breath I have.

There have been times when I did not know if I could carry on or sing another song, but every time God gives me what I need to accomplish what I need to do. He has never let me down! There have been times when I have got behind that microphone with only a third of my respiratory capacity, but all I have to do is open my mouth and begin to sing and God gives me whatever I need. God is a good God!

I have determined my heart and mind to go on, whether I sound good or not, feel good or not, accepted or not. And He will do the same for you. So, whatever worries you today, whatever dream you have, whatever desires you long to see fulfilled, give them to Him. He will surprise you.

7

Giving God Our Best

I believe as Christians we are called to continuous growth and maturity. When Jesus said in Matthew 5:48 'Be perfect, therefore, as your heavenly Father is perfect,' (NIV) the first mention of perfect was a reference to maturity and growth.

Perfection does not mean you will never mess up for we will not achieve total perfection until we see Him face-to-face. What it does mean is that we are called to be made more and more into His image and likeness.

Perfection is a maturing process that through our efforts of education, training, practice and all the things we do causes us to be the best we can be. It causes us to mature. As Christians we need to probe deeper into our creative abilities. We need to stretch ourselves and allow God to work through us.

Those of us who are parents know that fathers and mothers long for their children to grow, mature and develop into the best people they can be. God, as our Father, desires the same for us, His children.

Clearly, if this applies to every area of our lives, it also applies to our worship experience. We do not expect our pastor to preach the same sermon each week because we expect him to study, to get better and to mature. The same applies with worship and the worship team.

Our expressions of faith and worship unto God go through a maturing process. It is necessary for each of us to grow in our worship experience and not become stagnant. Anything that is not producing becomes stale and boring. It is lifeless after a while. The psalmist wrote time and time again about singing a new song to the Lord, about playing instruments and about giving God all of our heart. All those things are indicative of growth.

Let us look at all these references written by the psalmist. (Pay attention to the words in italics.)

Sing to him a new song; play skilfully, and shout for joy (Ps. 33:3).

He put a *new* song in my mouth, a hymn of praise to our God (Ps. 40:3).

Sing to the Lord a *new* song; sing to the Lord, all the earth (Ps. 96:1).

Sing to the Lord a *new* song, for he has done marvellous things (Ps. 98: 1).

I will sing a *new* song to you, O God; on the ten-stringed lyre I will make music to you (Ps. 144:9).

I will praise you, O Lord, with *all* my heart; before the 'gods' I will sing your praise (Ps. 138:1).

We must worship Him with all that we have, which is our best, and we should sing Him new songs, which indicates the need to develop new materials and new instruments, simply put—to grow!

A biblical example of growth in the area of worship can be seen when we compare Exodus 15 and 2 Chronicles.

'Then Miriam the prophetess, Aaron's sister, took a tambourine in her hand, and all the women followed her, with tambourines and dancing' (Ex. 15:20, NIV). The next verse goes on to say that Miriam sang to them. In this first biblical reference to a song of praise, we see how worship was born spontaneously out of a song Moses wrote thanking the Lord for His deliverance. There wasn't much practice or preparation involved in this 'worship service'.

Things were drastically different when Solomon dedicated the temple in 2 Chronicles 5-7.

All the Levites who were musicians—Asaph, Heman, Jeduthun and their sons and relatives— stood on the east side of the altar, dressed in fine linen and playing cymbals, harps and lyres. They were accompanied by 120 priests sounding trumpets. The trumpeters and singers joined in unison, as with one voice, to give praise and thanks to the Lord. Accompanied by trumpets, cymbals and other instruments, they raised their voices in praise to the Lord and sang: 'He is good; his love endures forever' (2 Chr. 5:12-13).

We see that the Israelites had come a long way from a few people playing tambourines. This was a huge procession, with tambourines, trumpets, other instruments and dancers. What had changed? The people had matured and grown in their worship experience!

Before I continue allow me to clarify one thing. I am not promoting pageantry or any given style of worship. Nor am I saying that only elaborate forms of worship are 'mature'. As you have already read part of my testimony, you know that my 'concert for One' took place in a small church, when it was only me and a piano I hardly knew how to play. Ultimately, worship is a matter of the heart.

But some people may argue that worship is only about the heart and that pageantry has no place in the church: I agree and disagree.

I believe that worship *is* a matter of the heart, and you can have the best band, the best dancers, the best banners, but if there is no heart-involvement you have nothing more than a show. On the other hand the Bible does not say anything against pageantry. God is an artist! If you want to see real pageantry just look at how beautiful and detailed this world is.

I want to be careful in saying this, because I know God will, and does, bless any genuine effort of worship, anywhere from one person playing guitar by themselves to a full-blown orchestra and choir. The issue arises when we use this as an excuse for not growing or maturing. I believe with all my heart that God longs for His people to develop not only individually but corporately.

A church that starts with thirty people and a pastor leading worship from a tape will eventually grow to sixty people and a guitar player or piano player. Someday that same church may have three hundred people and a small band. To me, it is all in the maturing. I am not saying every church is going to develop into a megachurch. But at whatever stage we are at we need to give God our best in order to mature and move on to the next step.

8

The Next Sep

In all my travels around the world I have seen maturity in people who give God their best in everything they have to offer. What is most fascinating is that even the people who have very little worship the Lord with a great passion and sincerity of the heart. The Lord spoke directly to me about this in Ghana, West Africa.

A few years ago I attended a conference in that country with eighteen pastors and a host of believers from the United States.

Like many of the others on the trip, I was realising one of the greatest desires of my heart—to minister the gospel of Christ in the homeland of my ancestors.

The host, Dr. Mensa Otibil, pastor of the International Central Gospel Church in Ghana, asked me to lead a special night of praise and worship and to deliver a word to the Christian singers and musicians in the city of Accra.

Leading praise and worship was something I was accustomed to, so I was glad for the opportunity. But how do you teach praise and worship to people who worship the Lord with a passion as intensely as anywhere I have ever seen in the world? It is like challenging Michael Jordan to a 'slamdunk' contest.

Still, I agreed to pray and seek God for a word to these people who sing, dance, pray and worship with an energy, effort and sincerity very seldom seen in modern Christendom.

I recognised that while I was highly moved by the excitement of the praise and worship I witnessed—not to mention the incredible potential I saw in the singers and musicians—their academic knowledge of fundamental music principles was lacking. Furthermore, most of the instruments were very poor in quality, and the sound system left much to be desired.

After much prayer, the Holy Spirit showed me something I believe is very important to all of us who are called to leadership in the praise and worship ministry: As we grow in our relationship and knowledge of God, we are also responsible to mature in the development of our expressions of praise and worship.

With this revelation, I began to study the Scriptures to see how the praise and worship experience progressed in its development and expression as the Israelites journeyed from the desert to the temple.

The Desert

Before the Exodus, Israel had been a people in bondage with no songs of praise on their lips and with no mighty works to sing about. They mourned and cried out to God about the conditions in which they lived.

It was not until God delivered them, parted the Red Sea and allowed them to cross in dry land that we find the first reference to them praising God in Exodus 15:20-21. After the Lord demonstrated His great power, Moses wrote a song recounting all God's great works. Miriam and the women took tambourines—probably the only instruments they had— and danced and sang the song that Moses had written.

At last! They had a song to sing. They had a Champion, a Deliverer, a God who had demonstrated a power greater than the power of the feared and awesome nation of Egypt.

God was pleased and received their offering of praise. They sang the only praise song they knew, the one that Moses had written. They rejoiced and celebrated as they recited the awesome works and deeds of their victorious Deliverer.

The Promised Land

In Joshua 6:2-5, as the Israelites faced their enemies in Jericho, the Lord gave specific instructions about how His people were to praise Him and allow Him to again show His mighty power and ability.

While they had seen many unusual things in their forty years in the wilderness, now they were called upon to do something highly irregular in terms of military strategy: quietly march around the city until their enemies were dizzy, and then terrorise them with music and shouts of praise until the walls of the city collapsed.

After crossing the Red Sea, they were given a reason to praise their God. Upon entering the promised land, they were taught the power of praise.

In the Jericho experience, five new elements were added to the experience of praise:

1. Obedience

The army was to carefully obey the commands of Joshua.

2. Order

They were to march around the walls six days without speaking a word. They were not to express any fears, doubts or complaints. (Remember, those were the reasons why their parents were not able to enter the promised land.)

3. Boldness

Without regard to what the enemy might think, the fighting men courageously positioned themselves in front of and behind the ark and the priests, demonstrating their trust and confidence in God.

4. Specific musical instruments

God called on His people to play the trumpet—a more sophisticated instrument than the tambourine—as they went into battle. Apparently playing the tambourine was not sufficient for the mission at hand.

5. Calling

The women sang and danced, but God called His fighting men to play the trumpets and shout praises aloud, declaring that the Lord had given them the city.

The Nation of Israel

The Lord again gave specific instructions about the types of instruments and singers that should accompany His presence in 1 Chronicles 15:16.

> David told the leaders of the Levites to appoint their
> brothers as singers to sing joyful songs, accompa-
> nied by musical instruments: lyres, harps and cym-
> bals.

All the people of Israel were invited to be a part of the processional celebration. And while King David and the priests learned that the presence of God (represented in the ark) was not something to be treated lightly or casually, everyone was now welcome to come into God's presence. It was during this period that offerings, sacrifices, costumes, music and dance were recognised as having a proper place in worship.

David went to great extremes to serve God with every gift and ability that he had, and he used the talents and skills of the people of the nation. Obviously, as the nation matured and developed, God expected His people to grow in their expression of worship to Him.

The Tabernacle

Once the ark was placed in the tabernacle, King David appointed skilled musicians to minister before the Lord on a regular basis (see 1 Chr. 16:4-6). By doing this he was letting the children of Israel know that praise and worship would no longer be an occasional event; it was to be a continual lifestyle.

David wrote songs and encouraged other skilled musicians and singers to write songs that glorified God. He challenged them not to be lethargic and lazy but to lift up their hands in the sanctuary and bless the Lord.

In the Mosaic tabernacle only the high priest had access into the holy of holies. But now, all of the priests who ministered in the sanctuary were able to enter into the presence of God.

The Temple

For the ceremony dedicating the newly completed temple (2 Chr. 5), King Solomon ordained great offerings and sacrifices. He commissioned the singers and musicians to produce and present the greatest processional the nation had ever seen.

Scripture says there were one hundred and twenty trumpeters, along with many appointed singers. Dressed in their priestly attire, they sang and played as one, proclaiming, 'For He is good, for His mercy endures forever' (v. 13).

The sanctuary then filled with a cloud—the awesome presence of God. No one was able to minister because the presence of the Lord was so overwhelming. When the people became as one in praise and worship to the Father, He came into their presence and allowed Himself to become one with them.

This 'becoming as one' did not just happen,

however. It took a great amount of deliberate effort. The Israelites had prepared a place for God's presence. The priests had sanctified themselves. They had studied the laws concerning the transportation of the ark. They had made offerings and sacrifices too great to be counted. They had prepared and composed music with excellent skill. After all of that, they became one before the Lord.

The Israelites persevered to the next step and drew closer to the Lord. In the desert, they learned how to *praise* God; in the battle at Jericho, the *power* of praise; as a young, growing nation, the *patterns* of praise; in the tabernacle the *priority* of praise; and in the temple, they became as one and experienced the *presence* of God through praise and worship.

That is my prayer for the church today. That is my heartbeat and passion. Read with me Jesus' prayer with reference to the power of unity, of oneness:

> My prayer is not for them alone. I pray also for those who will believe in me through their message, that all of them may be one, Father, just as you are in me and I am in you. May they also be in us so that the world may believe that you have sent me. I have given them the glory that you gave me, that they may be one as we are one: I in them and you in me. May they be brought to complete unity to let the world know that you sent me and have loved them even as you have loved me (John 17:20-23, NIV).

That is awesome! Think about it: when we become one with each other in Christ, we are then able to become one with God!

I believe that praise and worship is a God-given setting for His children to come together and fulfil the Saviour's prayer. When we join together in singing praises to the Father, we are able to transcend all doctrinal, cultural, racial and political boundaries and bring glory to Him.

If there is one thing I pray you have gleaned from this book so far it is the need to live in His presence. It is there you will find the fullness of Him—His power, love, mercy, grace and His desire for us to be united in purpose.

I have had the privilege to witness to people all over the world through worshipping the Lord with passion and intensity. I pray they will learn to praise God with increasing purpose, power and skill and become one before the Lord.

In fact, that is my prayer for all of us in the body of Christ: that we will sanctify our lives, overcome our divisions, give without measure, develop and offer our skills for the glory of God, and become one as worshippers of the most high God.

Perhaps then we will experience the presence of the Lord in a measure we have yet to know.

Section II

by Dick Bernal

Acknowledgements

I want to thank God for being the Father I never had, Jesus for sticking closer than a brother and the wonderful Holy Spirit for putting excitement into my Christian life.

Carla, you are one in a million. Thank you for being my wife, spiritual mother, friend and lover. What a woman!

To my three children, Adam, Sarah and Jesse, you bring unspeakable joy into my world.

To my staff and church—you are the best! Thanks to Larry and Melva Lea for the good and the tough times together in the fire. To Dr. Cho for being my pastor and mentor.

Thanks to Mike Hayes, Casey Treat, Steve Munsey and the gang at Integrity Leadership Ministries for speaking into my life and keeping me accountable.

Many thanks to Stephen Strang and John Mason for allowing Ron and I to do this project.

Thanks to Brian, Pat and the Jubilee worship team for stepping up to the plate week in and week out and delivering the 'goods' for God.

And last but not least, thanks to Ron and Tavita and the whole Kenoly family for entering our lives. You have enriched us beyond all words.

Introduction

With a handful of my friends and relatives I founded Jubilee Christian Centre in November of 1980. By 1985, it had grown to nearly two thousand weekly attendees. Things were going well in other areas of ministry, but Jubilee's services had fallen into a rut making times of worship dull. We needed someone to 'liven things up'.

Through a friend we met Ron Kenoly and invited him to sing a couple of songs for the dedication service of our new sanctuary.

When he came and began the worship service, we knew almost immediately he was the man for the job, and we hired him.

Ron and I developed a new style of ministry together. As we did this we rocked a few boats, and some people left the church. But at the same time our worship became real and powerful like never before.

In far too many churches professionalism and anointing are compromised for the sake of fellowship, cliques and family members. Many pastors are afraid to break the gridlock for fear of losing members, and they settle for mediocre worship.

That is not my style. I have found that by putting some basic principles about praise and worship into practice, a fresh anointing comes upon a church.

I have shared these with you in this book, but I am not prescribing a formula. As Ron often says, <u>there is no secret. You just follow the Holy Spirit.</u> May the Holy Spirit fill your heart with the joy and excitement of worshipping our King.

9

Recognising Praise and Worship

By nature, I am curious and a little analytical in my approach to life. I do not buy into things without first doing some research. Recently, when I was shopping for a fourwheel drive vehicle, I read books and articles, and questioned several four-wheel drive owners before I made a decision on the particular vehicle I wanted. The research helped me make a better educated choice.

I have also carefully studied praise and worship. I have found that there are a few differences between praise and worship. But both are necessary elements in a service, and both have their distinct qualities.

The Element of Praise

One of the Bible's primary themes is the human response to the reality of who God is. The examples of praise at such points in God's Word tend to be boisterous, joyful and spontaneous. It is illustrated by the response of the children of Israel when God rescued them from the Egyptians.

> Then Moses and the children of Israel sang this song to the Lord, and spoke, saying:
>
> I will sing to the Lord,
> For He has triumphed gloriously!
> The horse and its rider
> He has thrown into the sea!
> The Lord is my strength and song,
> And He has become my salvation;
> He is my God, and I will praise Him;
> My father's God, and I will exalt Him.
> The Lord is a man of war;
> The Lord is His name (Ex. 15:1-3).

Moses and the children of Israel had a new understanding of who God was. They discovered:

He is my strength.
He is my song.
He is my salvation.
He is my God.
He is my father's God.
He is a man of war.

This particular song written by Moses is referred to as a 'song of deliverance'. It is a praise to God for what He did for them. The children of Israel were headed for the wilderness and needed to learn how to praise their deliverer for His deliverance. Today, many of the songs we sing are praises to God for past deliverances and memorials to Him because He has never left His people.

So many times we forget our history. Praising God for what He has done reminds us that God is 'the same yesterday, today and forever!' (Heb. 13:8). If He did it once, He will do it again. The Latin word for praise means 'value' or 'price'. To give praise to God is to proclaim His worth. How we value God is how we will praise Him.

The summation of praise throughout the book of Psalms can be seen in Psalm 150:

Praise the Lord!

Praise God in His sanctuary;

Praise Him in His mighty firmament!

Praise Him for His mighty acts;
Praise Him according to His excellent greatness!

Praise Him with the sound of the trumpet;
Praise Him with the lute and harp!
Praise Him with the timbrel and dance;
Praise Him with stringed instruments and flutes!
Praise Him with loud cymbals;
Praise Him with clashing cymbals!

Let everything that has breath praise the Lord.

Praise the Lord!

This is a fitting conclusion to the 'book of praises'.
It also gives us a glimpse at the detail of the various
elements of temple music. Notice the sequence of
praise in Psalm 150.

Praise Him in the sanctuary
(church) (v. 1).

This is where most of us learn how to praise God.
Some things are taught and other things are caught.
You can catch a cold by just being around someone else who is infected with the virus. So too, you
can 'catch' praise by simply being surrounded by
'praisers'. This happens to me. Whatever I caught in

church I can still have in my car, office, home or anywhere. If I can praise Him on Sunday, why not on
Monday too?

Praise Him in His mighty firmament (v. 1).

Firmament speaks of the expanse of heaven (see
Gen. 1:8). God is bigger than my problems, bigger
than my church and bigger than my nation. Do you
get the picture?

Praise Him for His mighty acts (v. 2).

Once again we are reminded to remember His past
works, especially His intervention on our behalf.
Tomorrow's challenges are easier to face when we
remember yesterday's victories.

Praise Him according to His excellent greatness
(v.2).

We know where to praise God, now we are told
why we should praise Him. Praise is to be offered in
recognition of His great power and mighty deeds. His
creation, maintenance and redemption demand
praise. When we witness something powerful, we
automatically respond with, 'Wow!' A revelation of
the almighty, all-powerful One calls for nothing less.

Praise Him with (v. 3).

Our praise is enhanced when it is accompanied with instruments. Our entire being can become involved in the giving of praise to God. Our breath can blow air into an instrument or lift our voices in praise. Our fingers direct the sounds of instruments and our hands can beat the timbrel or clap in rhythm as our feet move in the dance.

All kinds of instruments can be used in worship. It is man and his traditions that limit usage. There isn't one instrument more holy or sanctified than another. The piano is no more righteous than the drums or electric guitar.

The Element of Worship

If praise is our response to His person, then worship is our response to His perceived presence. His presence transcends normal human activity, and it is holy.

> Then Jacob awoke from his sleep and said, 'Surely the Lord is in this place, and I did not know it.' And he was afraid and said, 'How awesome is this place! This is none other than the house of God, and this is the gate of heaven!' (Gen. 28:16-17).

Before Jacob's dream, '*this* place' was just '*that* place', as we see in Genesis 28.

> So he came to a certain place and stayed there all night, because the sun had set. And he took one of

the stones of that place and put it at his head, and
he lay down in that place to sleep.

An ordinary place was transformed into a holy
place because of the awareness of God's presence.
The presence of God had always been there, but Jacob
was asleep and oblivious to it. The consciousness of
God's presence brings forth worship. Worship will
manifest in many forms, yet it can be intensely private
and very personal. One may weep, kneel, pray, be
silent, lay prostrate or take on any physical posture
appropriate for the occasion. Worship music helps to
evoke deep passions and awareness that God is present. There is a tangible presence of which even my
flesh is aware.

In the story of Jacob, notice what took place after
his experience.

Then Jacob rose early in the morning, and took the
stone that he had put at his head, set it up as a pil-
lar, and poured oil on top of it. And he called the
name of that place Bethel (Gen. 28:18-19):

Jacob captured the moment by erecting a memo-
rial for others to enjoy. Even though worship is the
most personal and intimate of spiritual experiences, it
will flow out to others.

Real worship in a church service will touch the
hearts of the congregation. If we recognise praise and

worship we can come before the Lord as one. But before we can have 'real' worship we must understand the principles of it first.

10

The Principles of Worship

I have come to realise that God is not only a God of love but also a God of laws. He is known for His mercy and grace, but we cannot forget His principles and truth. In our modern society of political correctness, tolerance and appreciation of other's ideas, it is becoming unpopular to hold fast to the straight and narrow. Yet we are told in Proverbs 29:18, 'Where there is no revelation the people cast off restraint; but happy is he who keeps the law.'

Genesis, the book of beginnings, is our first glimpse of God and His ways. In Genesis, God addresses issues for the first time and sets precedents. Chaos became order when God spoke. Seedtime became harvest. Sin demanded blood sacrifice. Disobedience called for judgement. Faith brought blessing, and obedience never went unnoticed. These and other 'firsts' are set in principle and transcend dispensation. God's principles and truths are eternal.

Let us look at the first usage of the word worship in the Bible.

> And Abraham said to his young men, 'Stay here with the donkey; the lad and I will go yonder and worship, and we will come back to you' (Gen. 22:5).

This statement represented one of the most dramatic decisions in Abraham's life. God told Abraham to take his son to a mountain and to sacrifice him there. Abraham obeyed, telling his servants that he would go and worship.

The Lord is teaching us about true worship in Genesis 22. We must understand the principles of worship before we can add our voices, music and demonstration to the worship experience. In the following pages let's review five principles of worship as seen in the first twelve verses of chapter twenty-two.

1. Worship involves relationships—in this case, that of a father and son (vv. 1-3).

If our worship experience is right, it will be a relationship—one between you and the Father.

I was raised in a home that consisted of a grandmother, mother, two older sisters and a hard-working grandfather. My parents divorced before my second birthday, so the term 'father' meant very little to me.

As I grew older a tall, handsome stranger stopped by every few months for a visit. He called me 'son,' but I wasn't sure whether to call him 'Dad,' 'Daddy,' 'Pop' or 'Father.' He didn't seem to be very important in my life. I knew other kids had dads, but I did not feel that I needed one. I was well-loved by the family in my home.

The first day of kindergarten was traumatic for me. My grandmother walked me to school and waited in the room with the other parents as class began. Mrs. Tyson, my new teacher, asked each student to stand, give his name and tell the class what his father did for a living. Because I was seated at the back, I had several minutes to try to remember what my father did to make money. I had no idea! I barely knew *him*, let alone his vocation.

One by one, each student stood proudly and bragged about their own dad. As my turn approached,

I glanced at my grandma for help. I could see a look of concern on her face and could almost read her mind. 'Dickie, don't lie!' she seemed to say with her eyes. It dawned on me that I was different than the other kids. A feeling of shame, a sensation foreign to me, swept over me. I felt like running out of the room, but it was too late.

My friend Gary Goldman was sitting next to me. He stood up, and smiling from ear-to-ear said, 'My dad owns a garage.'

It was my turn. I peeked one last time at grandma, slowly rose to my feet and blurted out, 'My name is Dickie Bernal, and my dad owns a garage too!' Without hesitation I quickly sat down. It seemed an eternity passed before I dared to look at grandma. Her face read loud and clear, 'Wait until you get home, boy!'

Someone once said that worry is worse than fear because it gives you too much time to rehearse all that is going to go wrong. I rehearsed the details of my own impending doom as I walked home from school that day. Grandma came from the old school—the one that believed in woodsheds, paddles and lost privileges.

I arrived home and stood before her. Her skinny, little index finger accented her words. 'You ought to be ashamed of yourself, Dickie,' she told me. But I knew then that I would rather take a beating from her than have to endure the shame and embarrassment I felt in that classroom.

My problem grew along with me. As I participated in high-school athletics, friends would ask, 'Hey, Dick, is your dad coming?'

'Oh, he'll show up a little later. He's working late tonight,' I would lie. I created a fantasy world about my father to avoid facing the truth of my situation.

The problem didn't disappear when I accepted Christ as my Saviour. I identified with Jesus immediately when I came to him. He was a carpenter, and I was an ironworker. He was raised by a stepfather, and I had a stepfather. He liked to fish and so did I.

But I had a problem with Father-God. I had no idea how to talk to a father, so I had no idea how to pray to God. I could talk to Jesus, and I even got used to things of the Spirit, but Father-God was a confusing situation for me. I felt awkward and clumsy when I tried to relate to Him. I feared getting close to Father-God because I did not want to get hurt.

As a young pastor, I taught on many subjects relating to Christian living, but I ignored the fatherhood of God. God, who knew my dilemma, began wooing me during times of worship. I started having visions of Him not unlike Isaiah's vision of God in the sixth chapter of Isaiah. As He revealed His father-heart to me, I was finally convinced He would never leave me or forsake me. We formed a relationship.

Today I am no longer spiritually dysfunctional, lonely or in want. No, my father does not own a gas station—He owns the universe. I am not ashamed of His gospel for it has great power.

2. Worship involves a journey. Abraham and Isaac were going where God wanted them to go (v. 4).

Back in the sixties it was popular, especially here in the Bay Area, to 'trip out'. Many young people took mind-altering drugs to take them away from life's pain and struggles and to give them an artificial high. This was a dangerous and often fatal practice. It opened the door to the spirit world, and allowed demons to invade people's lives.

Worship is a pure 'high'. God is the Most High! Worship is a sanctified trip—a journey in the Spirit. Life with God is always moving in some direction.

For in Him we live and move and have our being (Acts 17:28).

The journeys of the children of Israel are recorded in the thirty-third chapter of Numbers. They camped, packed, departed and camped again nearly fifty times in this chapter. During these formative years in the wilderness, the children of Israel learned that life with God involves a lot of moving with intermittent stops along the way.

Our worship experiences can help us to move forward with God. Often people attending our worship services will express to me that they were *moved* by the presence of God in our worship. I have experienced the movings of God during worship; at times by a vision to a new avenue of ministry such as a trip to India or China; and at other times to a new level of growth such as when God recently showed me a vision of reconciliation between myself and a brother with whom I had been out of fellowship for years.

3. Worship speaks of *order*. The load of wood was taken off Isaac's back and placed carefully in order (vv. 5-9).

Jesus is the Alpha, the A, and the Omega, the Z, of our faith. But He is a God of order. Worship is order. We must travel from A to Z according to His order.

In the creation of the earth (see Gen. 1) we see order come out of chaos. The world we live in is chaotic, confusing, tempting, carnal and growing more perverted in every way with each passing generation. It is not popular or easy to live a life governed by principles, absolutes and boundaries. We must learn to bring the confusion of the world into the control of God.

Many a Sunday morning as I drove to Jubliee I felt like the 'Energiser bunny'—just keep on going!

Stressed out with enormous pressure from problems, I craved the moment I could enter His presence, lift up my hands to Him and by faith praise Him in advance for victory that would come.

Brokenness often precedes order. In the midst of one of King David's darkest moments, after Nathan the prophet had exposed David's sin before him (2 Samuel 12), he wrote the following words.

Wash me thoroughly from my iniquity, and cleanse me from my sin.

For I acknowledge my transgressions, and my sin is always before me.

Create in me a clean heart, O God, and renew a steadfast spirit within me.

Do not cast me away from Your presence, and do not take Your Holy Spirit from me.

O Lord, open my lips,

And my mouth shall show forth Your praise (Ps. 51:2, 10-11, 15).

4. Worship involves *sacrifice*. The story demonstrates Abraham's willingness to give up something precious and valuable (v. 10).

The Greek word for *sacrifice* is 'thusia', which primarily denotes the act of offering or that which is offered. It may be one's presence at church (Rom. 12:1), of faith (Phil. 2:17), money given for the cause of Christ (Phil. 4:18), spiritual sacrifices offered by believers as a holy priesthood (1 Pet. 2:5) or a sacrifice of praise.

> Therefore by Him let us continually offer the sacrifice of praise to God, that is, the fruit of our lips, giving thanks to His name (Heb. 13:15).

The verb form of *sacrifice* in the Greek is 'thuo'. It speaks of slaying or killing. To truly offer a sacrifice, death must come into the equation; death to pride, selfishness, greed, self-righteousness and other fleshly impulses. I had to die several deaths in order to come to church, come to Christ and answer the call to ministry—and I am not through yet. I have become fairly used to my own funeral services!

How well I remember the first time I lifted my hands in a worship service. I thought I would die of embarrassment, but I pressed on. Then there was the first time I danced in the Spirit. Me, a six-foot-two inch, 215-pound ironworker doing the Holy Ghost two-step. But once you put your hang-ups to death, they stay dead. Today it is natural for me to enter into worship—spirit, soul and body.

5. Worship opens the way for *provision*. God will provide through substitution (vv. 11-14).

Provision—the final product, but not until after the process. Abraham and Isaac went to the mountain to worship God. The process was painful, even agonising. It was a battle of fear versus faith. But what Abraham learned during the process made the provision that much sweeter.

Recently a local businessman gave 4.2 million dollars to Jubilee Christian Centre. It was a miraculous provision but a lengthy process preceded the miracle. Jubilee has sown millions into the mission field and other ministries for years, often to our own hurt. We went without our own building, adequate staff and television outreach so that we could help other ministries.

God remembered the process. He did not forget our labour of love, and one day His Spirit moved this businessman to give one of the largest one-time gifts in the history of the church.

It will be a journey. I am going where He wants me to go in the Spirit. Struggle and confusion will quickly be put in order. Sacrifice of praise will burst forth. A deep-felt willingness to die to self will

Finally, a fresh revelation of the power of resurrection will flood our souls, and we will easily celebrate Christ with all our minds, hearts and bodies.

11

The Tempo of Worship

Recently on a Monday morning, I sat in my office at home going over the previous day's services in my mind. The tempo was not right. It seemed jerky, like having stop signs on a motorway.

The worship had been exceptional. The high praises of God were filling the sanctuary. Hands were lifted; people were clapping; the sound of hallelujahs and amens could be heard throughout the service. Faces were beaming with the joy of the Lord.

As I reflected on the day, I recognised the point in the service when it felt as though the brakes were applied. It was when we greeted the visitors, proceeded with announcements and told several folks they left their headlights on. We also promoted the week's many services and activities.

I realised it was then the anointing left—and just in time for the offering. After the offering and the special music, it was time for me to give the message. At least fifteen minutes had elapsed since the end of our praise time. Because of that seemingly necessary time for church business, the congregation now needed a resurrection. It was time for the pastor to deliver the Word of the Lord, but the people had sunk back into the norm. This 'up-down-up syndrome' happens in most churches week after week.

I came to the profound realisation that God does not anoint announcements for jumble sales, three-minute skits to promote a retreat, bookshop discounts or any of the endless activities that take place in a thriving church community. All of these are already in the bulletin, so why do we overkill them? It's because we let our staff and department heads pressure us into being salesmen. When we do this the people become overwhelmed with facts and lose the spiritual lift from worship time.

I want to capture the anointing—not kill it. The worship team labours to welcome the presence of

God into a service, and we must not quench the Spirit with side issues.

The foremost important aspects of a church service are:

1. Praise and worship
2. The preaching of the Word of God
3. The altar call
4. The offering

If we could structure our services to connect these four parts without interruption, I believe we would see greater results. The level of intensity would remain high during the preaching segment and flow into the altar call for salvation, healing and deliverance. I believe the offerings would increase if people were challenged by the Holy Spirit instead of challenged by reports on the church budget. I have personally put this into practice at Jubilee, and the change was immediate and for the better.

I have visited Korea nine times. Dr. David Cho is my friend and pastor. Being a member of his board for Church Growth International, I am given a great opportunity to see his church (the world's largest church with seven hundred thousand members) up close. After all these trips and studies I have come to the conclusion that Dr. Cho keeps church simple and uncluttered. He stays focused on the priorities of his purpose and vision. I am doing likewise, although I have experienced times when the Holy Spirit will move outside the structure we plan on. I have found I need to be prepared for these times. In the story of David and Michal we find a great example of this.

Joy at Zion

David so craved the presence of God that he erected a simple tent to house the ark in Zion. He went to great lengths to bring the ark from the house of Abinadab to Zion (see 2 Sam. 6:1-19).

David was so excited that the ark now rested in the city of God that he cast off his royal garments and danced with joy in front of the people who were watching the procession enter the city. He humbled himself and came before his heavenly Father as a child who is overjoyed at the presence of his muchloved Dad. David's wife Michal was appalled. She rebuked David for his behaviour.

Michal represents the dignified crowd who become upset with those people who come to God as little children. As a result, God rendered her barren to the day of her death (see 2 Sam. 6:23). Churches that fail to produce born-again spiritual babies usually have the spirit of Michal in them. But being in God's presence was the most important thing to David.

As a pastor and teacher, I know the temptation to cut off a flow of His Spirit in a worship service because the eyes of my congregation are glued to the clock above the pulpit. At times, it is difficult for me to just let God have His way. But I am getting much better at recognising and responding to the Spirit's work because I hunger and thirst more than ever for His presence.

Today, as in the time of David, we must be careful not to balk at new things God may be doing.

Holy Laughter

When David returned the ark of the covenant to Zion (Jerusalem), his joy was so overwhelming that he was 'leaping and dancing before the Lord' (2 Sam. 6:16). Notice that when the people of Israel were released from captivity in Babylon and allowed to return to Zion another manifestation of joy occurred—'our mouth was filled with laughter' (Ps. 126:2).

This manifestation is occurring among believers today and we need to be prepared for it. Perhaps God is bringing us back to the joy of our salvation. Christians need a good laugh. At times the world sees us as rigid, boring and self-righteous. Often we even take ourselves too seriously. Our traditions and expectations lead us to create standards or laws that are impossible to live out in our daily lives. Thus we lose our joy and become dried-up spiritual prunes.

Does laughter have a place in church? Is it OK to laugh during praise and worship? Is it being irreverent or disrespectful to God or to the other people in attendance? This phenomenon is spreading around the world without a theological invitation. It has happened to me. Seemingly from out of nowhere, a sense of absolute euphoria hits you and you become really giggly, even if it is against your serious, conservative nature. Marilyn Hickey told me when it happened to her one night in a meeting, she ended up on the floor like a drunk lady. That seems totally out of character for her. But perhaps it's totally in character for God to release joy in our lives.

Do you remember the message from the angel to the shepherds on the night when Jesus was born?

> Now there were in the same country shepherds living out in the fields, keeping watch over their flock by night. And behold, an angel of the Lord stood before them, and the glory of the Lord shone around them, and they were greatly afraid. Then the angel said to them, 'Do not be afraid, for behold, I bring you good tidings of great joy which will be to all people' (Luke 2:8-10).

The angel did not say, 'Religion to the world, the Lord has come. Hey, shepherds, here is a new set of rules to keep you in check.' Nor , 'Joy to the church.' The angel announced, 'Joy to *the world*.'

Thousands of Americans are depressed to the point that they take some kind of medication to relieve their depression. The one place they should be able to go and find a reason to smile is the church, the house of God.

Jesus proclaimed a message of joy to the world. When He addressed the crowds of people on the mountainside, He said:

> Blessed are you who are poor, for yours is the kingdom of God. Blessed are you who hunger now, for you shall be satisfied. Blessed are you who weep now, for you shall laugh. Blessed are you when men hate you, and ostracise you, and heap insults upon you, and spurn your name as evil, for the sake of the Son of Man. Be glad in that day, and leap for joy (Luke 6:20-23, NAS).

I'm not suggesting that laughter is to be a part of every church service. As Solomon told us, 'To every thing there is a season, a time for every purpose under heaven' (Eccl. 3:1). In his list of things for which there is a season, he lists:

- A time to weep
- A time to laugh
- A time to mourn
- A time to dance (v. 4)

Recently a friend of mine told me, 'You must see the movie, *Forrest Gump*.'

When I asked why, he responded, 'Because it will

make you laugh, and it will make you cry. And, you'll feel good when you leave the theatre.'

I thought, *That is the way church ought to be*. We should experience a full spectrum of emotion which is touched by the Spirit of God. When we leave, we should be glad we came. And it is the pastor's job to see that the tempo of worship is constant so we can leave church feeling this way.

12

Setting Priorities for Ministry

I have had to ask myself, 'What is the main purpose of the local church?' I believe it is to provide a place for people to come and honour God through their presence, worship, tithing and willingness to serve.

Church is also a place for teaching, training and corporate praying. These functions result in a variety of ministries that spring up—everything from day care centres, Christian schools, Bible training centres, health clubs, restaurants and a host of special groups within the church community.

Jubilee is no different than any other large, growing church. We want to be relevant. We are very concerned about the family. I feel a mandate to reach young people and have just opened up what may be the largest Christian night club in the world, *Club J*. It will be an arm of evangelism to reach the hundreds of young people in this area. These kind of programmes are noble and good, but if I miss the basic reason for church, I need to go back over my priority list.

Over the years we have experienced a huge drain on the church general fund because of funding too many ministries. Once we had an elementary school with a monthly deficit of eight thousand dollars. We even had problems with the school objecting to our Sunday morning children disturbing the classrooms.

I realised that we were hurting our primary time of gathering on Sunday morning. Hundreds of children were being deprived of adequate classrooms because of our school. And it wasn't even a part of the original vision of our church. Unfortunately, I had listened to people instead of God when we established the school.

During this tough financial period, Ron came to me with a proposal to enhance our music department. We needed equipment, a new sound board and skilled musicians. We did not have the money because of our school. I had to make a tough decision— which was more important to the overall vision God had given to me?

There was no contest. The school had to go. Yes, many parents were upset—not to mention the teachers, but I had to do what was right. The whole church was being cheated of quality in worship because of one ministry which did not seem to fit into the vision for the total church. We relocated the children to well-established Christian schools that could provide them with a quality education, and it worked out for the best.

That whole ordeal taught me important lessons about keeping priorities straight. If I lose sight of those priorities then I am rendered useless to the body of Christ. There will be a breakdown of communication and ultimately, the vision for the church.

As I have learned to keep simple a structure at Jubilee the anointing in our worship time has continued to increase. People are being blessed and are coming into the joy of the Lord through His high praises and that is fulfilling the purpose of the church.

I believe an important priority is the quality of a worship service and what the worship team brings to it.

Should Musicians Be Paid?

When King Saul fell victim to dark, depressing

moods, his servants began a star search or talent hunt expedition to find a skilled player who could minister effectively to the king (see 1 Sam. 16:14-18). They did not just settle for whoever came along. They sought out a person with the best skills.

At one time in history, if you wanted to hear the best music and musicians in the world you went to church. That is not so today. Today you can go to concert halls, night clubs or casinos. The musicians are there because that is how they make a living.

I believe in voluntary help in church ministry. But I have re-evaluated my posture on church musicians. I now believe that certain skilled positions (piano, organ, guitarists or lead instrumentalists) should be paid to ensure that the best is present on Sunday morning. They may not be full-time employees, but they should at least be compensated for their gifts.

> For the kingdom of heaven is like a landowner who went out early in the morning to hire laborers for his vineyard. Now when he had agreed with the laborers for a denarius a day, he sent them into his vineyard. And he went out about the third hour and saw others standing idle in the marketplace, and said to them, 'You also go into the vineyard, and whatever is right I will give you.' So they went (Matt. 20:1-4).

How Much is Enough?

I am often asked, 'What is a fair salary or payment for a worship leader?'

One way to make this decision is to consider what you do with your worship leader Monday to Friday from 9.00 a.m. to 5.00 p.m. Do they travel to minister at other churches or functions? If so, do they keep the offering or is it deducted from their salary?

My personal philosophy about this is that the worship leader is one of the 'big three' —pastor, administrator/comptroller and worship leader. In California, these three individuals are often the highest paid members on a church staff. Both the administrator and worship leader are extremely important for the health and strength of a growing church.

At Jubilee we have several musicians on the payroll. These are skilled and necessary positions. Our budget is high for our music department, but our worship attracts thousands of people to Jubilee. It's a good investment.

If a worship leader has other skills such as counselling, computer skills, teaching and general pastoral gifts, they should be put on a full-time salary and provided a clearly defined job description. Schedule their office hours fairly, keeping in mind they are usually in attendance at every service.

At Jubilee, these individuals are scheduled Wednesday and Friday nights and three services on Sunday. They are also required to help with the crusades, conferences and seminars throughout the year.

I encourage a travelling ministry for our worship

leader. When Ron's popularity exploded internation-ally we sat down and discussed his ministry. We both rejoiced in God's plan. I did not fear losing Ron or the quality of worship in our church. If this was the Lord's doing, He would not abandon me and Jubilee.

Even now, Pure Joy (Jubilee's worship group) and Mark, Ron's brother, are ministering all over the United States. Do I keep them on the payroll? You bet! But if, like Ron, they are away more than they are at home, and their offerings sustain them, we will sit down and renegotiate their roles here at Jubilee.

Our church has always been a training centre for ministry. We have sent hundreds to Bible school, the mission field and other churches to help out. It is a calling on Jubilee to train, prepare and equip the saints for battle.

13

Worship and Spiritual Warfare

Teaching on the subject of spiritual warfare is one of my strong points. I teach about it regularly on my weekly international television programme. I have authored four books on the subject and teach it in churches around the world. It is a mantle God has placed on me and I do my best to walk in it.

I have discovered that <u>you cannot teach the</u>

dynamics of spiritual warfare by starting with silly little songs as a prelude to the message.

Ron and I have learned to work as a team when we travel in ministry together. His leadership in the worship services makes my job much easier. He prepares the congregation musically for what they will receive from the message.

Our signature scripture is Psalm 149 which defines the steps of worship we must take in order to prepare for spiritual warfare.

Sing unto the Lord a new song (v. 1).

This verse is talking about a fresh song—one that captures the 'now' move of God. I love the old hymns. Every now and then I take one out, dust it off and sing it to the Lord. That old hymn, be it from Luther or Wesley, was new at one time. It had a fresh anointing when it was birthed by God's Spirit. But for the most part, today it is a monument to what God did in days past. We should remember God's work in the past, but we should also keep up with what God is doing today. Then we will enable the congregation to 'rejoice in their Maker...and King' (v. 2).

Let them (v. 3).

Allow the congregation to worship God freely. I know there are eccentrics, show-offs and fleshly demonstrations which need to be monitored but not at the expense of quenching the Spirit. Nothing is more beautiful to me than someone expressing freely their praise to God by dancing in the Spirit.

One member of our church who came from a staunch Presbyterian background, came up to me excitedly one night to tell me what had happened to him during the service. This middle-aged professional man visited our church reluctantly with his wife a few months before. He enjoyed the service and continued coming regularly. He had never clapped, raised his hands or shouted to God during any of the services. He came mainly to keep peace with his wife.

On this particular evening, the worship service was especially powerful and passionate. My Presbyterian friend felt a warm glow all over him as he stood close to the back of the church. It flowed down from his head, and when it hit his feet, he got out in the aisle and danced unashamedly before the Lord with tears of humility running down his face. He had been set free to worship God as never before.

Let them sing aloud on their beds (v. 5).

We are told to take our worship home with us— even into our bedroom. Sing aloud on our beds? That's what happens in a real move of God. You worship at home, at work, while shopping or on holiday.

It sticks with you, and you have to share it with others.

> Let the high praises of God be...a two-edged sword in their hand (v. 5).

Now our worship turns to warfare. Our songs become the sword of the Spirit. These songs are prophetic in nature and perhaps spontaneous, on-the-spot songs. Ron is very gifted at singing a new song immediately after a sermon. Years ago, Reba Rambo McGuire prophesied that Ron would get a song from the Lord instantly after hearing his pastor minister the Word. This has been fulfilled in his ministry and continues to happen as he ministers today.

> To execute vengeance...and punishment on the peoples (v. 7).

Notice the increase of conflict.

> To execute vengeance on the nations, and punishments on the peoples; to bind their kings with chains, and their nobles with fetters of iron; to execute on them the written judgement—this honour have all His saints. Praise the Lord!

Jubilee has a local responsibility, as well as a national call, to remind people of the 'word of the Lord'. Every believer must be prepared to enter conflict with the enemy. This is not only a responsibility—it is an honour given to us from God (v. 9). This honour includes the binding of evil spirits (v. 8). The book of Ephesians tells us that the rulers we wrestle against are unseen, invisible ones, but they are as real as human rulers (see Eph. 6:12).

To execute on them the written judgement (v. 9).

I love this verse. The Bible is the ultimate written judgement of God. It is the final authority. The privilege of executing the Word of God to the world is not reserved for only those who are a part of the fivefold ministry (apostles, prophets, evangelists, pastors and teachers [see Eph. 4:11]), but for 'all His saints.'

Declaring God's Purposes

The Tiananmen Square massacre was one of the saddest events in the past several years, if not this century. Six months after the horrible incident, Ron, Carla and I were in Beijing with Nora Lam, Carolyn Sundseth (a former Reagan appointee) and Ruth Cox (a personal friend of President George Bush and his wife, Barbara).

Things were still very tense in Beijing at that time, and we could feel it in the air. I was given an historical opportunity to preach at the largest evangelical church in China, pastored by my dear friend, Pastor Kan. Until that time, our relationship had only been through the underground movement of Christians in China. It was a major breakthrough that I was allowed to speak openly at his church. I was told that Billy Graham was the only other American minister to have had this opportunity. I was the first charismatic to minister in this historical church.

The evangelical church movement is sanctioned by the communist government and tolerated as long as the people do not become too radical in their actions. President and Mrs. Bush attended the church while they served as ambassadors under President Nixon.

Pastor Kan gave me thirty minutes to do whatever I wanted. Before my message, Ron sang *Amazing Grace* and stirred the crowd. As Ron sang, the Lord whispered to me, 'Don't preach—just share your testimony.'

I moved along quickly from my prepared message to my personal story. The people laughed, clapped and cried. I did not hold back one bit. I told them Jesus and His baptism of fire were China's only hope. As I spoke I was able to identify several secret service agents who were in the crowd. The secret police in China are not very secret—their long, shiny, black leather coats stood out like a sore thumb. As I watched them, they appeared to be enjoying the service.

Later that day, as I entered Pastor Kan's office, he met me with an embrace. 'From the time my father pastored this church until now, this church has not experienced a move of God like the one this morning. In all those years, no one in the congregation has ever clapped their hands or laughed freely.' Pastor Kan was so overwhelmed that he continued hugging me for several moments.

The next day, Carolyn and Ruth were able to pull some strings to obtain permission to go out on Tiananmen Square. The deserted square was eerie with only a few soldiers marching around the perimeter. Martial law had been declared since the earlier demonstration. As we slowly walked out to the middle of the Square, we could still see the tread marks of military tanks and bullet holes in the pavement. The scene sent a chill down our spines.

We had brought with us some anointing oil that many of the saints in Pastor Kan's church had prayed over earlier. I opened the vial, poured it on the Square and led the small group of people in a prayer of repentance. We asked God to forgive the government of China for this terrible crime against her people, reminding God of His mercy and grace. At the end of my prayer, Ron began singing and led us in worship. We worshipped our Lord and proclaimed His ownership of all China. We served notice on Satan that his rulers had no power because Jesus had defeated him. We proclaimed that China would one day bow her knee to God.

Eight days later martial law was lifted in China. Today, China is opening her doors to the world slowly and will eventually be open to God.

When we returned to America, we brought Pastor Kan's daughter home with us. Our church is putting her through Bethany College of California in Santa Cruz. Pastor Kan has become the head of the religious bureau of China. I have a friend who will someday give me the green light to hold a massive crusade in the largest country in the world.

Breaking Satan's Yoke

Jesus has given us the legal right to use His name and power, but the legal right must be enforced. God's promises are not automatic. Salvation is available, but one must exercise faith to tap into it. The Bible is full of opportunities, but we must lay hold of them. Yes, Jesus disarmed the powers of darkness. But I cannot sit back and rest on His victory. I must daily enforce the truth of Calvary.

In the state of California there are traffic laws that determine the speed. It is law. It is posted. Yet we still have officers patrolling the roads. Why? If it is law, why waste time and money hiring patrol officers to enforce it. The reason is simple. Laws can be broken. It is the law of the universe that Satan has been defeated. It is recorded in the Book. It is posted. But Satan is not a law-abiding citizen. He is a criminal on the loose, and just because Jesus defeated him it is not enough to keep him from attacking us.

> You therefore must endure hardship as a good soldier of Jesus Christ. No one engaged in warfare entangles himself with the affairs of this life, that he may please him who enlisted him as a soldier (2 Tim. 2:3-4).

Spiritual warfare begins by the renewing of our mind. Then our families, churches, cities, nations and the heavenlies can also be renewed.

Overcoming Fear and Anger

Several years ago in 1990, my wife Carla and I witnessed to a young witch named Eric Pryor. After six hours, Carla led Eric to Christ. In the weeks to follow, we helped Eric relocate to San Jose and got him into a small, inexpensive apartment close to our church so we could disciple him. Someone donated an old car to Eric to commute back and forth to church.

Larry Lea and I, along with other prominent ministers in the area, held a Halloween night prayer rally in San Francisco in October of 1990. We did not intend to stir up any trouble from the gay and occult communities of San Francisco, but on the night of our rally, over three thousand angry homosexuals, lesbians and witches gathered outside the civic auditorium to protest. They kicked, spat at and harassed

Christians as they arrived for the rally. The atmosphere was explosive.

Eric, Carla and I travelled together to the rally. The protestors cheered when they saw Eric emerge from the car because he was well-known by many people in the crowd. But they grew silent when Carla and I stepped up beside him. We were the oddest of trios. My dear friend Dr. Peter Wagner told me this was one of the most significant clashes of good and evil in the past fifty years.

Out of this night of prayer and spiritual warfare the spiritual climate over the bay area was altered for the better. We are experiencing a unity among churches here like never before in the two hundred year history of the evangelical church in the bay area.

Was there a backlash? We had no idea that event would be covered by the media locally, let alone internationally. But it hit the front pages of our local newspapers and of the *Wall Street Journal*. It was broadcast on CNN and by NBC radio nationwide. *Current Affair*, *Inside Edition, Montel Williams* and even a newspaper from Paris wanted live interviews.

It was the catalyst for a national broadcast on *Prime Time Live*, where Diane Sawyer took a swipe at what she called questionable claims by religious leaders. Both Larry Lea and I suffered greatly for three years with problems on both personal and public levels. We paid the price but held our ground, and God has come through for His servants. Eric is still with me, and he is serving God with all his heart.

The Sunday morning after the programme aired on national television, I drove to church depressed, discouraged and defeated. I wondered how I would be able to worship God with all my heart wondering who the congregation believed—their pastor or the press. Ron knew the turmoil I was going through, and he 'turned it up a notch' during the worship service that Sunday morning in November. As a result, I was able to overcome my fear and anger at the personal attack against my ministry, and I felt God's strength refresh and empower me anew.

Praise Binds Fear

As a kid growing up in a small town I enjoyed nothing more than catching an afternoon matinee at the Fox Theatre.

During the late autumn and early winter months, we would leave the show around 5.00 p.m. and walk three to four miles home. We threw rocks, kicked tins, raced and played tag on the way. It was usually dark before we got there. About halfway home, we would pass through an old cemetery. No one ever said much, but we all whistled and looked as cool as we could. That graveyard always gave me the 'willies', and somehow the whistling brought a feeling of peace.

Fear is a tormenting force. It grips and grinds on one's soul. Fear is simply the feeling of losing something or someone, the fear of losing one's life, family, career, youth, reputation or anything precious to us. It also carries the definition of 'flight in terror'. We get the term, *phobia*, from the Greek word *phobo* found several times in the New Testament. Fear, being one of the great stiflers of faith, was the first fruit of disobedience by man.

> Then the Lord God called to Adam and said to him, 'Where are you?' So he said, 'I heard Your voice in the garden, and I was afraid because I was naked; and I hid myself (Gen. 3:9-10).

Fear is no respector of people. It comes to us all in many packages. Over and over the Bible commands us to 'fear not'. Even David battled fear in his life.

> I am forgotten like a dead man, out of mind; I am like a broken vessel. For I hear the slander of many; fear is on every side; while they take counsel together against me, they scheme to take away my life (Ps. 31:12-14).

But remember in the twenty-third psalm David also wrote:

> I will fear no evil; For You are with me; Your rod and Your staff, they comfort me (v. 4).

I remember being afraid of the dark. I would lay in my bed at night and hum a little tune to bring peace to my soul. Today as a middle-aged man I still wrestle with fears, but I bring them to God. No more humming a made-up tune for hours at night. Now I can sing of His praises and bind fear knowing that God is with me. He has the power to bring peace to the troubled waters of our souls.

14

The Role of Music in Worship

Not long ago while driving home from work, I put the radio on scan. I am not sure what I was looking for, but suddenly I heard an 'oldie' from the fifties that I had not heard for more than thirty years, yet I knew every word in the song. I sang along with the artist like I had just memorised the tune yesterday. It brought back memories of junior high school, high school hops, old friends and an age of innocence.

I don't know of anything as nostalgic as music. Advertisers offer collections of tunes from the 40s, 50s, 60s and 70s. Psychologists suggest it to their patients to calm them from the daily stress of life. And couples in love memorialise their relationship in the words of 'their song'.

Some time ago a member of our congregation asked, 'Pastor, why is it so hard to memorise scripture, yet I know all the songs we sing by heart?'

'I'm not sure,' I responded. 'But why don't you make up a little melody for the verses you want to memorise and see what happens?'

Advertisers have understood the power of music for years. I can still sing little jingles I learned from Grandma's black and white television back in the fifties—from Alka Seltzer to Ford motor cars.

The Lord, fully understanding the power of music and memory, instructed Moses to teach the children of Israel a song.

> Now therefore, write down this song for yourselves, and teach it to the children of Israel; put it in their mouths, that this song may be a witness for Me against the children of Israel. When I have brought them to the land flowing with milk and honey, of which I swore to their fathers, and they have eaten and fllled themselves and grown fat, then they will turn to other gods and serve them; and they will provoke Me and break My covenant.

Then it shall be, when many evils and troubles have come upon them, that this song will testify against them as a witness; for it will not be forgotten in the mouths of their descendants, for I know the inclination of their behaviour today, even before I have brought them to the land of which I swore to give them.' Therefore Moses wrote this song the same day, and taught it to the children of Israel (Deut. 31:19-22).

The Lord knew His people would backslide, and the best way for them to remember His Word was with song. The thirty-second chapter of Deuteronomy records the 'Song of Moses'. It was one of his last acts for God. It covered a time from Adam to the present and into Israel's near future. It said it all!

Many times after I finish preaching, Ron comes up with a new song that encapsulates my message. One message, titled 'From A to Z', takes me forty-five minutes to deliver. But Ron came up with a catchy little tune and a reggae beat to go along with the message soon after I first delivered it. People may not remember every detail or point of my sermon, but they leave church singing that song.

Years ago, my brother-in-law owned a country and western saloon called the Silver Saddle. Soon after his conversion, he allowed me to bring a gospel singer to perform, along with a group of Christians to pass out tracts and witness to the patrons. By the time we started, most of the locals were already drunk and rowdy. As the singer sang praises to God and we passed out tracts to the crowd, they cursed at us, hooting and hollering.

A few became nasty and left, but most of them stayed. Eventually the crowd calmed down and actually began listening to the music. Soon people sitting at the bar began yelling out, 'Hey, sing *Amazing Grace* or how about *The Old Rugged Cross*?'

One half-drunk lady sang every word as tears streamed down her face. 'I haven't sung that song in fory years,' she exclaimed.

Before closing time in the saloon that night many prayed with us. Later, they demanded my brother-in-law have gospel night at least once a week, but he was anxious to please God with his life and sold the bar. Today, it has become a thriving church in Morgan Hill, California.

Lucifer in the Church

There is an old saying, 'When Lucifer was cast out of heaven he landed in the choir loft!' Usually a frustrated pastor will be the person quoting it. Whatever causes a rift or disunity between the worship leader and the pastor opens the door to the 'Lucifer spirit'.

In Ezekiel, a lamentation against the king of Tyre is given. Many scholars believe this is a direct reference to Satan (Lucifer). Many Old Testament verses contain such dual reference.

> Son of man, take up a lamentation for the king of Tyre, and say to him, 'Thus says the Lord God:
>
> 'You were the seal of perfection,
> Full of wisdom and perfect in beauty.
> You were in Eden, the garden of God;
> Every precious stone was your covering:
> The sardis, topaz, and diamond,
> Beryl, onyx, and jasper,
> Sapphire, turquoise, and emerald with gold.
> The workmanship of your timbrels and pipes
> Was prepared for you on the day you were created'
> (Ezek. 28:12-13).

Lucifer was unique—beautiful to behold and beautifully adorned. He was talented and musical, but he was created.

He was perfect in his ways. Who would not hire this guy? He could do it all! He was able to lead, administrate, organise, stir up and he was obviously tremendously anointed. He also wasn't bad to look at. Most pastors would probably trip over themselves to put him up in front of the people. However, iniquity was in his heart. He had his own agenda.

He had a bad case of the 'I wills', instead of being interested in what his leader wanted (see Is. 14:12-14). This is the root of most problems between the pastor and the worship leader.

Lucifer had forgotten that God created him. His problem came through 'the abundance of your trading' (Ezek. 28:16). Lucifer was trading with the other angels of God in the heavens. He actively engaged in swaying others to revolt against God. And he is still doing that today.

Could it be that Lucifer began to listen to the praises of certain angels, and the praise went to his head? 'O, Lucifer, you're so beautiful, so talented.' His influence was so great that as many as one-third of the angels left heaven with him in the first church split. They must have believed he was greater than God. In reality, he wanted to be their god.

The mantle of authority and leadership within a church rests on the senior pastor. All other staff members have been called by God to assist the senior pastor. This is true of worship leaders also. It should be necessary for worship leaders to go over songs and arrangements for a service with the pastor to make sure the service flows in unity with the music. This will help keep a good line of communication open between the two and not open any doors for the Lucifer spirit to enter in.

The Bennetton Church

Jubilee Christian Centre is represented by several different cultures and ethnic groups. I am often asked, 'How do you draw such a diverse ethnic mixture?'

This blend was no accident or surprise. Carla and I set out to have a culturally diverse church. Years ago, we had a vision for such a church.

At an early age I learned to appreciate culture. My best friends were Hispanic, black, Jewish and oriental. I 'cross-pollinated' easily. Perhaps that is one of the reasons Jubilee is the way she is today.

My right hand man, Larry Hayashida, is Japanese; Pastor Ron, Brian Waller and Ellis Carter are black; my head elder is Korean; my secretary is Hispanic and—well, you get the picture—Jubilee is a real rainbow coalition. We target our worship to reach not only the various cultures but each generation as well. We want to reach the 'Boomers', the 'Xers' and everyone from the fourteen-year old boy to the ninety-year-old grandmother.

Northern California, especially Silicon Valley, is a microcosm of the peoples of the world. I want to reach the gang member, the yuppie, the second- and third-generation Latino, the struggling young couple and the homosexual who is desperately trying to break free from his bondage. I know there has to be power in our worship service because it's the first thing these people are going to experience. Without wilfully trying to offend the older, traditional crowd, we keep the sound up and intense. And for the most part, we sing 'new songs' to the Lord.

Sing to Him a new song;
Play skilfully with a shout of joy (Ps. 33:3).

Following my instructions, Ron or Brian will begin
a worship service with the choir singing one or two
contemporary songs to welcome the people, get them
seated and in the Spirit. Then we crank it up for ten
minutes or so of hand-clapping, footstomping, happy-
but-militant music.

After this the worship leaders move into slower,
softer worship songs which lead people into a hum-
ble, prayerful mood. During this segment of the service many come to the altar and kneel or prostrate
themselves before the Lord. Finally, we move into a
time of reflection, with time for tears of joy and repentance.

At times we will include a traditional hymn at this
point. By the time we conclude, we have celebrated
God—the One who is 'high and lifted up'—and
made our worship personal by acknowledging His
presence within us (Is. 57:15).

Thus, we have gone from heaven to our own heart
in about twenty minutes. The last song we sing takes
the worship back up to a level of high intensity. We
try to find a song that fits that morning's message. By
the time I stand to preach, it is not uncommon for me
to be standing before a crowd spiritually on fire. I do
not have to watch the clock during worship. If the

congregation seems to want to worship longer, I will trim my thirty-five minute sermon back to twenty-five or thirty minutes just to let the people celebrate Christ and His resurrection.

There have been Sundays when I was unable to preach because the flow of the Spirit during worship was so strong that I just could not stop worshipping—nor did I want to. Not long ago I had prepared a 'humdinger' of a message. I hardly slept, and I was so excited to get to church. But God was more excited about being worshipped than about hearing my message. We had a 'Holy Ghost runaway', and over one hundred and fifty people received Christ into their lives that Sunday morning.

The move of God's Spirit can sweep over a worship service at any time—and in any way He chooses. The Spirit is not bound by tradition or schedule. When a congregation touches the very heart of God with praise and worship, He responds by filling the hungry hearts of people with His presence and power.

Many pastors are praying for revival, for a great move of God within their churches. Many Christians are longing for God to reveal Himself in a new and fresh way. Enter into the high praises of God. Do not be afraid that God will move in a way you cannot predict or choose. Come into His presence in unity, desiring only to open yourselves to His Spirit. Acknowledge His presence in your midst. Celebrate Him.

Music can pave the way into the very heart of God. Worship Him in your music, and bask in the joy of an intimate celebration of His love.

15

Worship—God's Glue for The Body

Recently we held our 8th Annual Worship Seminar at Jubilee Christian Centre. Worship International, an outreach of Hosanna Integrity Recording Company, co-hosted this year's event. Nearly one thousand worship leaders and pastors from all over America attended the seminar. Friday night was a praise and worship service which was open to anyone who wanted to attend. Even though we set up every extra chair that we could find, our two-thousand seat sanctuary was filled to capacity. People stood in the foyer and flowed out into the car park just to be part of our worship experience.

Ron led an all-star team of singers and musicians in a two-hour worship experience that night. A large number of Baptists, Presbyterians and other mainline Evangelicals were registered for our conference, yet that evening everyone attending was worshipping God with uplifted hands, singing and dancing in the Spirit. No one left offended or confused.

Many people from more conservative camps seemed to flow right along with us. Towards the end of the service, Ron asked people who needed ministry to come to the front. People from all walks of life came forward. Other Christians prayed, laid hands on them and prophesied words of encouragement. Although I could tell this experience was a first for many people, they loved it. People are hungry for a touch from the Father.

Worship seems to be the glue that God is using to keep us together as a body. Even though the words of many praise songs contain strong theological statements concerning faith, healing, warfare and prosperity, singing the words seems to be more palatable than hearing these doctrines delivered in a sermon.

One major challenge facing worshipleaders is knowing how to introduce this kind of worship to their own churches.

The Shepherd Leads the Sheep

Once, a pastor's wife asked, 'Dick, how did you convince your elders to hire Ron, a black man, whose style and background was so different from you and your church?'

'Sister,' I responded. 'God is a God of theocracy not democracy. He always dealt with a man or a woman, not with a committee.'

I continued by sharing my philosophy of leadership with the seminar attendees. I am a leader who leads—I am not a hireling. I was called by God to lead my congregation. The rest of the leadership team was called to follow the vision given to me by God, and spoken and expressed by me to our leaders.

This is the way leadership was expressed in God's Word. God spoke to the leader—be it Adam or Noah, Abraham or Moses, David or even Jesus. Then they led helpers to come alongside and assist in the vision.

There is only one vision at Jubilee, and it is God's. My best advisors are my pastoral team. I make decisions based upon their counsel. I do not call for a vote from the elders or from the congregation. My pastoral team knows more about our church and our people than a businessman who visits the church on Sunday and wants to vote on every issue at the Monday night board meeting. It is the pastor-shepherd's job to lead the sheep—not for the sheep to lead the shepherd.

Moses experienced some difficulty with the first principle of worship.

> Then Miriam and Aaron spoke against Moses...So they said, 'Has the Lord indeed spoken only through Moses? Has He not spoken through us also?' And the Lord heard it. (Now the man Moses was very humble, more than all men who were on the face of the earth.) Suddenly the Lord said to Moses, Aaron and Miriam, 'Come out you three, to the tabernacle of meeting!' So the three came out. Then the Lord came down in the pillar of cloud and stood in the door of the tabernacle, and called Aaron and Miriam. And they both went forward. Then He said, 'Hear now My words:
>
> If there is a prophet among you,
> I, the Lord, make Myself known to him in a vision;
> I speak to him in a dream.
>
> Not so with My servant Moses;
> He is faithful in all My house.
> I speak with him face to face.
>
> Even plainly, and not in dark sayings;
> And he sees the form of the Lord.
> Why then were you not afraid
> To speak against My servant Moses?'
>
> So the anger of the Lord was aroused against them, and He departed (Num. 12:1-9).

In this instance, God intervened on Moses' behalf. Miriam became leprous for her disloyalty to Moses, her leader. It was only after Aaron repented, and Moses prayed for her healing that God restored her health. As a reminder to her of her disloyalty to Moses, she was shut outside the camp with the other lepers for seven days (v. 32).

The elders and deacons in a church must understand their responsibilities according to the Word of God. The senior pastor is the shepherd and should rise up with strong leadership and a clear vision from God for his church. The anointing of God rests on him—he wears the mantle of leadership.

> But my horn You have exalted like a wild ox;
> I have been anointed with fresh oil (Ps. 92:10).

In the King James version the word *unicorn* is used. The psalmist may have been referring to the aurochs, a horned wild ox so large and powerful that no one could control or tame it. The Hebrew word for wild ox or unicorn is *reem* which comes from the word *raam*, meaning 'to rise' or 'to be lifted up'.

The ninety-second psalm is called a 'psalm (song) for the Sabbath Day'. The writer is telling us they have been anointed with fresh oil, and because of it, their horn (strength) is lifted up or exalted like the strength of the wild ox.

The wild ox was created by God to be free to live the way God made him. His power and strength were admired by one and all. Our churches need a fresh anointing of God's power and His presence. Pastors need to be delivered from the fear of man and of public opinion. Strong leaders build strong churches, and strongholds are torn down. The responsibility of the elders and deacons of a church—and of the congregation—is to support and assist the pastor in fulfilling his vision from God.

The Pastor's Participation in Worship

One Sunday at lunch after a great service, Ron and I and several other people sat around a table discussing that morning. As we talked, Ron broke into the conversation and said, 'Pastor, you sure make my job a whole lot easier by the way you worship. When they see you entering into worship it is so much easier for me to lead them into worship too.'

His statement caught me off guard, so I asked him to explain what he meant. 'The congregation watches everything you and Carla do up on the platform,' Ron continued. 'Especially the way you worship.'

This is especially true for men. Women seem to enter into worship easier and quicker than men do. Their emotions connect much faster with the move of the Spirit. Men process and reason all the hows and whys over most issues—including our spiritual experiences. We are much more likely to have a 'wait and see' attitude. Our pride, ego and upbringing dictate a certain aloofness when it comes to expressing a real heart-felt emotion.

Carla finds it quite natural during a worship service to lift her hands, cry, shout, clap and dance at the drop of a hat. In the past, there were times when I would get a little embarrassed at her freedom and think, 'There's just no way this salt-and-pepper-haired, dignified pastor is going to get into all that.' I was always a six-foot-two-inch, 215-pound, ex-construction worker, bullrider, karate instructor, man's man. My type does not dance before the Lord—not in private, or, let alone, in front of thousands. I have had to learn to worship God freely and openly.

One Sunday morning years ago something gripped my pride and insecurity and shook it loose. I found myself acting giddy and foolish, and I didn't give a hoot what anyone thought. To my surprise, many of the men in the congregation joined in with me, much to the delight of their praying wives.

Ron helped me to understand that no matter how hard he works to lead people into a freedom of worship in Jesus, if I look stiff and uncomfortable, it speaks volumes to the crowd. If I am the spiritual leader of the church and I am not enjoying worship, then why should the people enter in? If I want Ron to help me prepare the people for the ministering of

God's Word through my teaching gift, the least I can do is help him minister to the Lord through his music gift. A worshipping church must have a worshipping pastor.

Free the Load

Recently I spoke in a church in Dallas, Texas. The pastor shared with me a story about ancient camel drivers. Camels were, and are, a primary source of transportation in the Middle East. The camel drivers had a command, 'Galal!' At this loud command the camels would kneel down or roll over on their sides so their master could unload or 'free' the load. Obviously, the camels were glad to get the burden off their backs. How many of us are carrying loads we need to give to God?

Peter spoke of a way to unload our burdens in 1 Peter 5:6-7:

> Therefore humble yourselves under the mighty hand of God, that He may exalt you in due time, casting all your care upon Him, for He cares for you.

In the book of Matthew, Jesus spoke of unnecessary religious works as burdens men are forced to carry.

> The scribes and the Pharisees sit in Moses' seat. Therefore whatever they tell you to observe, that observe and do, but do not do according to their

works; for they say, and do not do. For they build heavy burdens, hard to bear, and lay them on men's shoulders; but they themselves will not move them with one of their fingers (Matt. 23:14).

The early church leaders recognised the importance of avoiding the heavy burdens and cares that could prevent spiritual growth. They advised the gentile converts in Antioch, Syria and Cilicia:

For it seemed good to the Holy Spirit, and to us, to lay upon you no greater burden than these necessary things (Acts 15:28).

Worship can be the vehicle by which we lay our heavy burdens at the feet of Christ. People enter our sanctuary confused and discouraged. They are beat up by the world, depressed, troubled and double-minded. Yet as they begin to bask in His presence and lift their heavy hands heavenward the burdens of the week are slowly lifted off their weary backs.

Our Master in heaven is giving the command 'galal' to us on earth.

Kneel down, turn over, let Me untie this great load and free you from the cares of this world.

As we respond to the command we will discover it is the quickest way to enter into worship and praise to the Father.

16

The Prophetic Nature of Worship

As a pastor and teacher, I pride myself on my discipline to prepare. My most important function is to bring a fresh, strong, applicable word every time I step into the pulpit. I prepare notes to have in front of me, and it is my intention to stick to my outline as I speak. But my personality is spontaneous. Our most memorable services were those when I was moved by the Spirit and spoke as He directed, ignoring my notes.

At times I have found it necessary to listen to a

tape of the message in order to know what I said during a prophetic unction or declaration that was not in my notes. Through the Spirit I may have issued mandates and decrees, challenged the powers of darkness, addressed the angels or even reminded God Himself of His promises. The anointing is an awesome thing, and while it rests upon you, you feel the surge of the Holy Spirit moving in power within.

A young prophet and dear friend, Kim Clement, comes to Jubilee frequently. Kim brings with him his own worship leader. At first I was offended by this. I thought it was like bringing a sandwich to a banquet. This is Jubilee! The home of Ron Kenoly and Pure Joy. The Jerusalem of church worship.

I changed my mind quickly the first night Kim ministered at our church. Israel, his worship leader, ministered in song and on the keyboard right along with the young prophet. Israel would break into a spontaneous song right in the middle of a point Kim was making. We would join in as a church and sing a prophetic unction to our city. This happened several times during the service. It was spontaneous, free-flowing and very exciting.

Kim shared the difference between normal church worship and spontaneous proclamation. Basically, a normal worship service is well-orchestrated and predictable. For the most part the people know what to expect. No interruptions are allowed.

During a time of spontaneous worship there can be time for a word from the Lord, a call for the needy to come forward for ministry or a period of waiting on the Lord for renewal. Both Ron and Brian are opening up to this new flow of spontaneous worship. I believe many worship leaders desire to experience such freedom in their worship services. It elevates the congregation beyond 'canned' worship experiences. Such worship is too predictable.

> Oh, sing to the Lord a new song! For He has done marvellous things; His right hand and His holy arm have gained Him the victory. The Lord has made known His salvation; His righteousness He has openly shown in the sight of the nations.
>
> He has remembered His mercy and His faithfulness to the house of Israel; all the ends of the earth have seen the salvation of our Lord. Shout joyfully to the Lord, all the earth; break forth in song, rejoice, and sing praises (Ps. 98:1-4).

How Worship Prepares You for the Prophetic

Ron and I agree that most church services are somewhat constricted to a time schedule by nature. This is not all bad. People need to have some frame of reference as to the length of the service. In fact, the number one question visitors ask is, 'How long is the service?'

In order to stop limiting a move of the Spirit, I have offered a Friday night service, which I call, 'Practising the Presence of God'.

When we were a part of the lifestyle of the world, we gave no thought to time when it was time for a party. Our activities were spontaneous, free and exciting. Our worship to God should also provide spontaneity, freedom of expression and excitement.

Our Friday night services are casual and relaxed. We come ready for a visitation from God. I rarely prepare a sermon, preferring to stay open to an 'on the spot' *rhema* word from heaven. I may read a psalm, quote a scripture or give a testimony, but the emphasis of the evening is upon worshipping and waiting on God. This type of service can become spiritually intoxicating.

> And do not be drunk with wine, in which is dissipation; but be filled with the Spirit, speaking to one another in psalms and hymns and spiritual songs, singing and making melody in your heart to the Lord, giving thanks always for all things to God the Father in the name of our Lord Jesus Christ, submitting to one another in the fear of God (Eph. 5:18-21).

My gift of prophecy blossoms under this style of free-flowing ministry unto the Lord. Usually the Lord points out individuals who need a 'word in due season'. I am by nature a reluctant prophet. I wear this mantle, but I wear it uncomfortably. Yet, when I come under the anointing I move rather boldly and clearly. I believe the heavens open when unrestricted praise is offered up to our Father.

It is very important that the worship leader and musicians move in the same flow, or they could quench the move of the Spirit. Ron knows how to segue with me as changes come to the service. Our relationship is so close, especially in the spirit, that we work together like a hand in a glove.

> But now bring me a musician. And it happened, when the musician played, that the hand of the Lord came upon him (2 Kin. 3:15).

Kim Clement has gathered a covenant group of musicians to travel with him to enhance his prophetic gifting. Ron and I have learned a lot by watching Kim. One night at our church, he kept the worship service at a fever-high pitch for well over an hour. At dinner late that night I asked Kim why he did that.

He responded, 'There was great territorial resistance in the heavenlies tonight because of the word I was to deliver to you and this church. I couldn't minister the word until we broke through with praise. Once I felt the darkness lift I was released to give a prophetic utterance.'

Discernment is vital to understanding the move of God. Without it, it would be possible to misunderstand what God is trying to say to His people. In fact, it would be possible to completely miss the move of God.

God often moves in unexpected ways. In the sixteenth chapter of Acts, we find Paul and Silas imprisoned in a cold, dark cell. Yet their circumstances did not hinder them from entering into a time of praise and worship where they broke through the territorial resistance resting over that prison. As they sang and praised God, God moved in an unexpected way—through a great earthquake. No one recognised that moment for what it was except Paul and Silas.

> But at midnight Paul and Silas were praying and singing hymns to God, and the prisoners were listening to them. Suddenly there was a great earthquake, so that the foundations of the prison were shaken; and immediately all the doors were opened and everyone's chains were loosed. And the keeper of the prison, awaking from sleep and seeing the prison doors open, supposing the prisoners had fled, drew his sword and was about to kill himself. But Paul called with a loud voice, saying, 'Do yourself no harm, for we are all here' (Acts 16:25-28).

Because of that supernatural move of God, the keeper of the prison and his whole family were saved. As we enter into the freedom of praise and worship, the dark clouds of resistance which Satan uses to blind our eyes to the moving of God will lift. We will be able to discern what God is doing and how we can be a part of His move. His presence will fill our lives with His *rhema* word, just as His presence filled Solomon's temple as the Israelites praised and worshipped God.

> Indeed it came to pass, when the trumpeters and singers were as one, to make one sound to be heard in praising and thanking the Lord, and when they lifted up their voice with the trumpets and cymbals and instruments of music, and praised the Lord, saying: 'For He is good, for His mercy endures forever,' that the house, the house of the Lord, was filled with a cloud (2 Chr. 5:13).

> Then Solomon said: 'The Lord said He would dwell in the dark cloud' (2 Chr. 6:1).

One Friday night in 1984 I had a close encounter with God. Carla and I were struggling personally and corporately with finances. In fact we had sold our house and given the money to the church to pay its bills. I felt guilty moving my family into a smaller rental home, but they all agreed it was for a just cause.

I had carefully prepared a message I believed our church needed to hear. It dealt with some of the challenges of the day, especially in our fellowship. Everything began normally as we sang familiar songs and enjoyed God's presence. Then suddenly Dr. Gene Flood, a Stanford University professor, began shifting the service from the keyboard of his Hammond B-3 organ.

As he played, people filled the aisles and began to dance before the Lord. Some of them had never danced before, and I was amazed by what I was seeing. It was as though a giant dose of joy had fallen on all.

I felt giddy, my legs buckled under me and I fell down. I fought to keep my composure, but the more I fought the more drunk in the Spirit I became. I remembered what it felt like to be intoxicated in the world.

The service continued in this way for more than two hours. Eventually, the ushers carried me to my car. I assured them I was able to drive. It was about 10.00 p.m. when I headed home. I had only travelled two miles when a policeman pulled me over. I bowled over in laughter.

Two large officers approached me, one on each side of the car. One officer had his hand on his holster, ready to draw his sidearm if I became dangerous.

'Are you OK, sir?' the officer on my side asked as he shone a torch in my face.

I tried to explain what had happened, but I could see their suspicion. Finally I said, 'I'm the pastor of a church close by. We just had one wild service, and I'm intoxicated on the Holy Spirit.'

They stared at me without blinking an eye. As they

looked round my car, they saw my Bible, teaching tapes, worship tapes and other church stuff.

One officer broke into a grin. 'Well, pastor, do you think you can stay on the road?' he asked. 'We pulled you over because you were swerving.'

'I'm fine, guys. Really, I'm just great. Thanks!' I responded. I was fine. God had ministered to me in a strange yet powerfully new way that night.

God longs to reveal Himself to His people in unique and powerful ways. As we learn to praise Him with our whole being He will come and dwell in the midst of our praise. As God meets us in the midst of praise, we will echo the words of David:

> My praise shall be continually of You...And [I] will praise You yet more and more (Ps. 71:6, 14).

God inhabits the praises of His people.

His presence is intoxicating. His presence is liberating. His presence is empowering.

Epilogue

Ron Kenoly and Dick Bernal have helped us to understand the power of praise. They have shown us that as we express ourselves through music in our praise we can be transported into the very heart of God. That is the place we need to be. There we find the strength to leave behind the encumberances of life that hinder us from becoming one as worshippers. There we defeat the enemy, disarming the powers of darkness and living victorious Christian lives. There we receive a fresh anointing that will fill our lives as the cloud of God's presence filled the temple sanctuary. There we become the temple of God that He intends for us to be.

When Jacob awoke from sleep where he encountered the awesome presence of God, he exclaimed, 'Surely the Lord is in this place, and I did not know it' (Gen. 28:16). That ordinary place on the side of the road was transformed into a holy place.

The sanctuary, the temple, became a holy place because of the presence of God. That can happen to us. Keep lifting Him up. Let Him lift you into His presence to be transformed from an ordinary people into a holy people.

Worship with Ron Kenoly

Sing Out With One Voice

Ron Kenoly's latest release features a 350-voice choir, orchestra, dancers, banners, the African Children's Choir and much more. Includes: *Oh, the Glory of Your Presence*, *Sing Out* and *Ain't Gonna Let No Rock*.

God is Able

Features the 120-voice Atlanta Praise and Worship Choir. Includes: *Use Me*, *The Battle is the Lord's* and *His Eye is on the Sparrow*.

Lift Him Up

The all-time best-selling Hosanna! Music album. Includes: *Lift Him Up*, *Ancient of Days* and *Let Everything That Has Breath*.

Jesus is Alive

Ron's first Hosanna! Music album, recorded live in San Jose, California. Includes: *Jesus is Alive*, *Making War in the Heavenlies* and *Hallowed Be Thy Name*.

Ron Kenoly's music is available on cassette, CD and backing tracks. Except for *Jesus is Alive*, all albums also have videotaped versions. Ask for these products in your local Christian bookshop.

If you would like to correspond with the authors you may contact them at:
Jubilee Christian Centre,
175 Nortech Parkway, San Jose, CA 95134, U.S.A.